WANDERLUST BUCKLIST SERIES

DESTINATION ARIZONA

Travel Guide, Adventure Game Plan, and Wish List

John Christopher Lee

Table of Contents

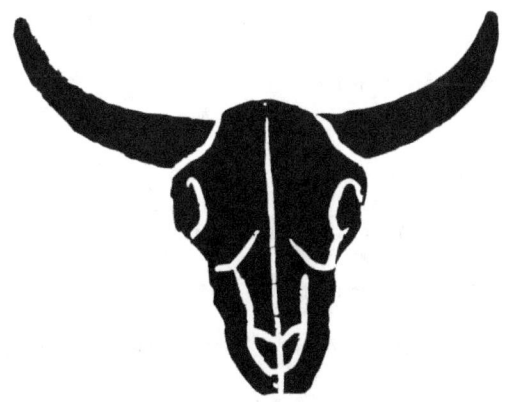

INTRODUCTION

Have you ever stood on the edge of a canyon so vast it seems to stretch into eternity, with colors so vivid they appear to be painted by the hand of an artist? Or wandered through a desert that comes alive with blooming wildflowers after a rare rain? If you haven't, let me tell you—Arizona is unlike anywhere else.

Arizona is a land of contrasts. From snow-capped peaks to sun-scorched deserts, ancient cultures coexist with vibrant modern cities. This isn't just a state; it's a journey through time, nature, and human ingenuity. There's magic here—something about how the sunsets paint the sky in fiery oranges and purples, how the saguaro cacti stand tall like silent sentinels, and how the air smells fresh and wild. Arizona doesn't just offer adventures; it provides transformation.

The Allure of Arizona

Arizona is a state that defies expectations. Take the Grand Canyon, for example. No photo can capture the way the light shifts and dances across its layers of rock. Standing on its rim is a humbling experience, a reminder of how small we are in the face of nature's grandeur.

But Arizona isn't just about its famous spots. There are countless hidden gems for every well-known destination—places you can only find by veering off the beaten path, conversing with a friendly local, or taking a chance on a dirt road.

And then there's the culture. Arizona's history is as rich as its landscapes. From the ancient cliff dwellings of the Ancestral Puebloans to the vibrant art scene in Sedona, there's a story behind every corner. Native American heritage is woven deeply into the fabric of the state, and you'll find opportunities to learn about it everywhere—from museums and guided tours to festivals and traditional ceremonies.

Best Times to Visit and Seasonal Highlights

Arizona is a year-round destination, but knowing when to visit can make all the difference. In the spring, the desert blooms come alive with color, and the weather is perfect for hiking. Conversely, fall brings cooler temperatures and a golden glow to the aspens in Northern Arizona.

Summer, while hot, isn't off-limits—it's the perfect time to explore higher elevations or cool off at one of the state's many lakes. In winter, you can ski in Flagstaff in the morning and enjoy a sunny hike in the desert in the afternoon. Few places offer that kind of versatility.

Journey Awaits

As you embark on your Arizona adventure, know you're stepping into a world of endless possibilities. This isn't just a trip; it's an invitation to connect with nature, history, and yourself in ways you never imagined. Whether you're marveling at the majesty of the Grand Canyon, exploring a ghost town, or simply watching the stars in one of the state's many dark-sky parks, Arizona has a way of staying with you long after you've left.

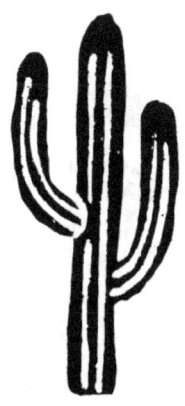

CHAPTER 1

Northern Arizona Wonders

"In every walk with nature, one receives far more than he seeks."
—John Muir

Northern Arizona is a land of breathtaking contrasts and absolute beauty. It is where ancient history meets modern adventure, where the earth reveals its secrets through majestic canyons, windswept mesas, and towering peaks.

Whether you're seeking awe-inspiring landscapes, cultural experiences, or the kind of adventures that make your heart race, this region offers it all in abundance. Let's start our journey in one of the most iconic destinations in the world—the Grand Canyon National Park.

Exploring the Grand Canyon National Park

If there's one place that truly defines the essence of Northern Arizona, it's the Grand Canyon. No matter how many photos you've seen or stories you've heard, nothing can prepare you for the moment you stand on the edge of the South Rim and take in the vastness of this natural wonder.

The Grand Canyon is not just a place you visit; it's a place you experience. The South Rim is a perfect starting point with its sweeping views and well-maintained trails. Begin your journey at the Grand Canyon Visitor Center, where you'll find maps, exhibits, and knowledgeable staff ready to help you plan your day.

If you're up for a stroll, the Rim Trail offers spectacular views without requiring strenuous effort. For a deeper dive, the Bright Angel Trail provides an unforgettable trek into the canyon's depths.

But the Grand Canyon isn't just about its iconic views. It's also a haven for adventure seekers. Guided rafting trips range from half-day excursions to multi-day adventures that immerse you in the canyon's wild beauty.

For a more serene experience, consider a mule ride along the canyon trails. These gentle giants have safely transported visitors through the Grand Canyon for over a century. Riding a mule down the narrow, winding paths is exhilarating and offers a unique perspective on the canyon's immense scale.

Beyond the trails and vistas, the Grand Canyon is a treasure trove of history. The Desert View Watchtower, designed by architect Mary Colter in 1932, is a tribute to Native American artistry. You'll find murals that tell the story of the region's indigenous peoples.

You should consider a guided tour of the Grand Canyon. Whether it's a ranger-led hike, airplane-guided adventure, or a helicopter ride over the canyon, having an expert by your side can add context to your experience.

The Grand Canyon is a place to be savored. Sit on the rim with a journal, take in the view, and let the grandeur of this natural wonder seep into your soul.

Antelope Canyon and Horseshoe Bend Adventures

There's magic in the way light dances. You'll find this magic in Antelope Canyon, where the sun's rays transform narrow sandstone walls into glowing, dreamlike passages. Located just outside Page, Arizona, this slot canyon is one of the most photographed places in the world—and for good reason.

Your adventure begins with a guided tour, the only way to access the Upper and Lower sections of Antelope Canyon. As you step into the canyon, the walls, sculpted by centuries of wind and water, curve and twist in almost otherworldly ways. In the Upper Canyon, shafts of sunlight stream down from above, creating surreal patterns and illuminating the rock's reds and oranges. The Lower Canyon, narrower and more challenging to navigate, offers equally stunning views with a slightly more adventurous twist.

But it's not just the visuals that make Antelope Canyon unique. It's the feeling. There's a profound stillness here, a sense of being enveloped by nature's artistry.

A short drive away is Horseshoe Bend, a breathtaking overlook of the Colorado River as it makes a dramatic 270-degree curve. This iconic site, often called the "East Rim of the Grand Canyon," is easily accessible via a short hike from the parking area. Be prepared for a bit of a climb—though it's not overly strenuous, the desert sun can make it feel more challenging.

When you reach the overlook, the view is spectacular. Standing on the cliff's edge, you'll see the emerald-green river far below, framed by red rock cliffs that stretch forever.

If you visit around sunrise or sunset, you'll see an even more incredible sight. The changing light bathes the canyon in a golden glow, and the shadows add depth and drama to the scene. This is a bucket-list location for photographers, so bring your camera and take your time capturing the perfect shot.

Antelope Canyon and Horseshoe Bend are deeply connected to the Navajo Nation, and visiting these sites offers an opportunity to learn about the region's rich cultural heritage. Many of the guides who lead tours through Antelope Canyon are members of the Navajo community, and they share stories and insights that add a deeper layer of appreciation to the experience.

Monument Valley and Navajo Tribal Park Insights

There's a reason Monument Valley feels familiar. Its iconic sandstone buttes and sweeping desert landscapes have graced countless movies, TV shows, and advertisements, becoming synonymous with the American West. Nothing compares to experiencing this sacred place in person.

Nestled within the Navajo Nation, Monument Valley is a stunning natural wonder and a place steeped in history and culture. As you approach the valley, the towering red rock formations seem to rise out of the earth, their stark beauty contrasting with the desert sky.

Your first stop should be the Monument Valley Navajo Tribal Park Visitor Center. From here, you'll get your initial glimpse of some of the valley's most famous formations, including the Mittens and Merrick Butte. These iconic rock formations are a photographer's dream, especially during sunrise and sunset when the light casts long shadows and paints the desert in vibrant hues.

The best way to truly immerse yourself in the valley is by taking a guided tour led by a Navajo guide. These tours offer access to areas off-limits to the general public, including ancient ruins, petroglyphs, and sacred sites. The guides share stories and legends passed down through generations, giving you a deeper understanding of the land and its significance to the Navajo people.

For a more adventurous experience, consider hiking or horseback riding in the valley. The Wildcat Trail is the only self-guided hiking trail in the park, offering a closer look at the Mittens. On the other hand, horseback riding allows you to channel your inner cowboy or cowgirl as you explore the desert landscape.

Monument Valley is also rich in cultural experiences. If you have the chance, attend a Navajo cultural event or demonstration. From traditional hoop dancing to rug weaving, these events provide a glimpse into the vibrant heritage of the Navajo people. And don't leave without trying fry bread—a delicious staple of Navajo cuisine.

While it's easy to get lost in the grandeur of the landscape, remember that Monument Valley is more than just a beautiful backdrop—it's a living, breathing part of Navajo history and culture. Treat it respectfully, and you'll walk away with more than stunning photos. You'll leave with a connection to the land and its people, that will stay with you long after your visit.

Flagstaff and the Scenic San Francisco Peaks

Flagstaff is the kind of place where the Old West meets modern adventure. Nestled at the San Francisco Peak bases, this charming mountain town is a gateway to Northern Arizona's most breathtaking natural wonders. But don't let its small-town vibe fool you—Flagstaff is bursting with personality, outdoor activities, and a rich history that begs to be explored.

Driving into Flagstaff, you'll notice the towering peaks dominating the skyline. These are the San Francisco Peaks, sacred to many Native American tribes, including the Hopi, Navajo, and Zuni. Humphreys Peak is 12,633 feet, the tallest point in Arizona. If you're up for a challenge, hiking to the summit offers incredible views and a sense of accomplishment that's hard to beat.

For those who prefer a less strenuous adventure, the Arizona Snowbowl is a fantastic destination. It transforms into a snowy playground for skiing and snowboarding in the winter. But even in the warmer months, the Snowbowl offers scenic chairlift rides that provide panoramic views of the surrounding forests and valleys.

Downtown Flagstaff is a delightful mix of old and new. Historic Route 66 runs right through the heart of town, and you can't miss the vintage signs and classic diners that harken back to a bygone era. A favorite spot is the Weatherford Hotel, a historic landmark with a cozy bar and a rooftop patio perfect for soaking in the mountain air.

Flagstaff is also an outdoor enthusiast's paradise. The nearby Coconino National Forest boasts diverse landscapes, from ponderosa pine forests to red rock canyons. The Lava River Cave, a unique underground tube formed by ancient volcanic activity, is a must-visit for anyone with a sense of adventure. Bring a flashlight and sturdy shoes—it's dark and rugged.

If you're traveling with family, the Lowell Observatory is a hit for all ages. Known as the place where Pluto was discovered, this observatory offers interactive exhibits and nightly stargazing programs. On a clear night, the telescopes give you an up-close view of planets, star clusters, and galaxies. It's a humbling reminder of our place in the universe and a great way to end a day of exploring.

What makes Flagstaff truly special, though, is its community. The locals are friendly and passionate about their town and their infectious love for the area. Whether grabbing a coffee at a local café or joining a group hike, you'll feel like part of the Flagstaff family in no time.

So, as you explore Flagstaff and the San Francisco Peaks, take your time to savor the unique blend of history, adventure, and natural beauty. This is Northern Arizona at its finest—where every corner holds a story, and every trail leads to a discovery.

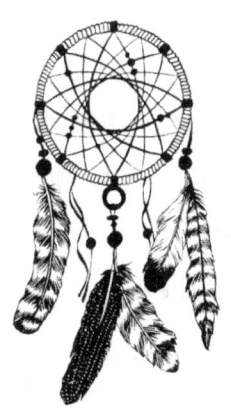

CHAPTER 2

Sedona's Spiritual Vibes and Red Rock Wonders

"Sedona is a cathedral without walls. It is a place where the earth speaks to you, and the sky listens."
—Unknown

Sedona isn't just a destination; it's a feeling, an experience, a place that captures your soul and invites you to explore its stunning landscapes and yourself. Nestled in the heart of Arizona, Sedona is renowned for its red rock formations, vibrant art scene, and legendary energy vortexes.

Sedona offers the answer if you've ever wondered what it's like to stand at the intersection of natural beauty and spiritual wonder.

The towering sandstone cliffs, painted in shades of crimson and gold, seemed to glow under the sun while the surrounding juniper forests filled the air with their earthy aroma. But there's something more to Sedona than meets the eye. Locals and visitors speak of a unique energy that pulses through the region, a magnetic pull that draws people in and changes them.

Introduction to Sedona's Energy Vortexes

When people think of Sedona, the term "energy vortex" often comes to mind. The concept of energy vortexes stems from the belief that certain areas on Earth are natural power centers where energy is either entering or leaving the ground. In Sedona, these vortexes are said to amplify your energy, making it a hotspot for meditation, healing, and self-discovery. Some visitors report feeling a sense of calm and clarity, while others describe a physical sensation—a tingling in their hands or a warmth in their chest.

Sedona has four main vortex sites: Cathedral Rock, Bell Rock, Airport Mesa, and Boynton Canyon. Each one has its unique energy and personality.

Exploring these vortexes isn't just about standing at a specific spot—it's about immersing yourself in the landscape. Take the time to hike the trails, sit quietly, and let the surroundings speak to you. Even if you don't experience anything "energetic," the sheer beauty of these locations makes the journey worthwhile.

One tip is to go early in the morning or late in the afternoon. Not only will you avoid the crowds, but the changing light creates a magical atmosphere, with the red rocks glowing as if lit from within.

For those looking to dive deeper, consider joining a guided vortex tour. Many local guides are well-versed in these sites' history, geology, and spiritual significance. Some tours even incorporate meditation or yoga, enriching the experience.

Cathedral Rock and Bell Rock Hikes

If Sedona had a crown, Cathedral Rock and Bell Rock would be its jewels. Their stunning beauty and accessible trails make them a must-visit for any Sedona adventurer.

Let's start with Cathedral Rock, one of Sedona's most famous formations. The trail to Cathedral Rock is short but steep, a 1.2-mile round trip that rewards you with jaw-dropping views. As you climb, you'll navigate red rock ledges and scramble over boulders, each step bringing you closer to the breathtaking summit. The energy here is palpable—this is one of Sedona's main vortex sites, and many hikers pause at the top to meditate or soak in the serenity.

At Cathedral Rock, the sky turns shades of orange and pink, casting a warm glow over the rocks and the valley below. Moments like these make Sedona feel genuinely magical.

Next, let's discuss Bell Rock. Located just south of Sedona, It is another vortex site and a popular hiking destination. Unlike Cathedral Rock, Bell Rock offers a variety of trails, ranging from leisurely strolls to challenging climbs.

A great trail is the Bell Rock Pathway, a 3.6-mile round trip that loops around the base of the rock. The views are spectacular, with Bell Rock towering above and Courthouse Butte nearby. You can scramble up Bell Rock for the more adventurous, though the ascent can be tricky.

The Best Scenic Drives Around Sedona

Driving through Sedona is like stepping into a painting. The red rock formations rise dramatically against the blue sky. Whether you're a seasoned road-tripper or just looking for a leisurely drive, Sedona's scenic routes are guaranteed to take your breath away.

One of the most famous drives is the Red Rock Scenic Byway, Highway 179. This 7.5-mile stretch of road is often called a "museum without walls," and it's easy to see why. As you wind through the valley, you'll pass landmarks like Bell Rock, Cathedral Rock, and the Chapel of the Holy Cross. There are plenty of pullouts along the way, so take your time and stop to soak in the views.

Another must-drive route is Oak Creek Canyon, often referred to as the smaller cousin of the Grand Canyon. The 14-mile stretch of Highway 89A between Sedona and Flagstaff is a beautiful drive. You'll wind through a lush canyon, with towering cliffs on either side and the sound of Oak Creek flowing below.

If you're feeling adventurous, consider exploring Schnebly Hill Road. This rugged, unpaved road takes you high into the mountains, offering panoramic views of Sedona and the surrounding wilderness. I'll warn you, though—it's not for the faint of heart. A high-clearance vehicle is a must, and the road can be rough.

Sedona's Art and Cultural Scene

Sedona isn't just about stunning landscapes—it's also a hub for creativity and culture. The town's vibrant art scene is a reflection of its natural beauty and spiritual energy, drawing artists and craftspeople from around the world.

One of the best places to explore Sedona's art scene is the Tlaquepaque Arts and Crafts Village. A Mexican-style village is home to galleries, shops, and studios showcasing everything from fine art to handmade jewelry. Strolling through Tlaquepaque is like walking through an artist's dream.

Also, visit the Sedona Heritage Museum. Housed in a homestead, the museum offers a glimpse into the lives of Sedona's early settlers.

Sedona is also known for its festivals, including the Sedona International Film Festival and the Sedona Arts Festival. These events bring together artists, filmmakers, and creatives from around the globe, making Sedona a cultural hotspot.

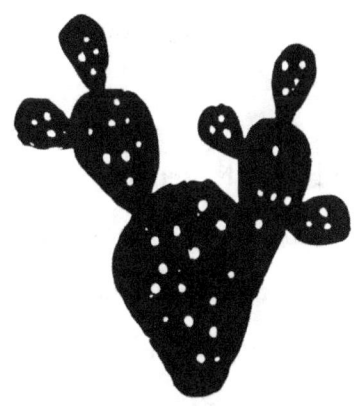

CHAPTER 3

Phoenix and the Valley of the Sun

"Phoenix is not just a city; it's a desert oasis that rises, shines, and surprises with every visit."

Phoenix, Arizona, is a city that pulses with energy, sun, and a rich blend of history and modernity. Nestled in the Valley of the Sun, Phoenix serves as both Arizona's capital and the American Southwest's heartbeat. As the fifth-largest city in the United States, it stands as a testament to resilience, having transformed from a dusty desert outpost into a vibrant urban landscape.

When you think of Phoenix, images of vast desert landscapes, towering cacti, and scorching sunshine may come to mind. But what you might not know is that this desert city is brimming with culture, outdoor adventure, and an eclectic food scene.

Exploring Downtown Phoenix and Its Museums

Downtown Phoenix is a dynamic blend of the old and the new, where historic landmarks stand side by side with modern architectural wonders. The downtown area is filled with life, from its lively streets to its impressive arts and culture scene. Whether you're a history buff, an art lover, or simply someone who enjoys exploring a city's beating heart, downtown Phoenix will not disappoint.

One of the first places to visit is the Heard Museum. This museum focuses on Native American culture, history, craftsmanship, and traditions. The Heard Museum's exhibits are thought-provoking and beautifully curated. There's a deep sense of respect for the people and stories told here, and it's a must-see for anyone visiting Phoenix.

And the Phoenix Art Museum should also be high on your list. It's the largest art museum in the southwestern United States, and walking through its halls is like embarking on a global art tour. You'll find works spanning centuries and continents, including European masterpieces, contemporary art, and diverse exhibitions that reflect the cultural richness of the region.

Phoenix's downtown is also home to the Arizona Science Center, which is perfect for families and anyone with a curious mind. The interactive exhibits make science fun and accessible to all ages, with a focus on space, technology, and the natural world.

Another standout spot in downtown is Roosevelt Row, a trendy district filled with art galleries, independent shops, and murals that create a colorful, almost bohemian atmosphere. You could spend hours strolling through this neighborhood, taking in the sights and sounds of this creative enclave, and you'd still find new spots to discover.

Hiking in South Mountain Park

If you're the kind of traveler who loves a good adventure, hiking in South Mountain Park is something you absolutely must do. This park is one of the largest municipal parks, and it offers an extensive network of hiking and biking trails that wind through the rugged desert landscape, providing stunning views of the city and the surrounding mountains. The park is expansive—more than 16,000 acres of desert terrain, offering everything from easy strolls to more challenging summit hikes.

A favorite trail is the Holbert Trail, which leads to the top of a mountain saddle and offers panoramic views of the valley below. It's a challenging hike, but the sense of accomplishment at the summit makes it all worth it.

Another popular trail is the National Trail, a longer, more strenuous route that takes you deep into the park's natural beauty. Along the way, you'll encounter desert flora, including saguaro cacti, creosote bushes, and palo verde trees. Also, you might spot rabbits, birds of prey, or even a desert tortoise if you're lucky.

South Mountain Park is not only about hiking, though—it's a great place to explore the region's unique desert environment. The park is home to Native American petroglyphs, remnants of ancient rock art created by the Hohokam people. These petroglyphs are scattered across the park, offering a glimpse into the area's history and culture.

There are also scenic drives and bike paths that allow you to experience the park's beauty at a slower pace. The Dobbins Lookout offers a breathtaking view of the valley and is a perfect place to catch a sunset or take in the city's sprawling landscape.

Regardless of the trail you choose, South Mountain Park is an essential part of the Phoenix experience. It's a place where you can connect with nature, enjoy a little exercise, and take in some of the best views the city has to offer.

Day Trips Around Phoenix

While Phoenix has plenty to offer, the surrounding area is just as remarkable. There's no shortage of day trip options that allow you to explore the natural wonders and hidden gems of Arizona.

The Desert Botanical Garden. Located just outside the city, this 140-acre garden is a sanctuary for desert plants. Walking through the garden feels like stepping into another world, where vibrant flowers bloom against the backdrop of the desert's rugged terrain. The garden's trails take you through a variety of ecosystems, each showcasing the diversity of the desert's plant life.

One of the highlights of the Desert Botanical Garden is the opportunity to experience the landscape's changing colors and textures as the sun shifts throughout the day. It's a photographer's dream, and whether you're a professional or an amateur, you'll find endless inspiration here. The garden is also home to art installations, seasonal events, and educational programs that give visitors an understanding of the desert's delicate ecology.

For something a little different, consider taking a day trip to the nearby town of Jerome. Once a thriving copper mining town, Jerome is now a quirky, artsy destination perched on the side of a mountain. The town offers stunning views of the Verde Valley and is home to galleries, shops, and a fascinating history museum. Jerome is also known for its ghost tours—if you're into the supernatural, this town is said to be one of the most haunted places in Arizona.

Another great day trip option is to head north to Sedona. Just a two-hour drive from Phoenix, Sedona offers spectacular red rock formations, hiking trails, and vortex sites that attract visitors from all over the world. The drive itself is beautiful, taking you through the high desert landscape and into the heart of Arizona's geological wonderland. Once you're in Sedona, you'll find plenty of hiking, art galleries, and spiritual experiences that are truly unique to this area.

For a more historical experience, a visit to the town of Prescott is a wonderful option. This charming town, with its Victorian-style buildings and historic courthouse, offers a glimpse into Arizona's past. Prescott is also home to several outdoor activities, including hiking, fishing, and boating on Watson Lake.

The Best Local Food and Shopping Spots in Phoenix

No trip to Phoenix is complete without indulging in its food scene and exploring its eclectic shopping options. Whether you're craving a gourmet meal, looking for local artisan goods, or shopping for southwestern treasures, Phoenix delivers.

For breakfast or brunch, head to Matt's Big Breakfast, a local institution known for its mouth-watering dishes like corned beef hash and waffles. The restaurant has a casual, no-frills vibe, but the food is top-notch, and the portions are generous. Another great spot for breakfast is The

Hash Kitchen, which serves up creative dishes like the "Hashini" and a variety of build-your-own Bloody Mary options.

Phoenix is home to a thriving Mexican food scene, and you can't leave without trying the local fare. Barrio Cafe, a colorful and vibrant restaurant, serves some of the best Mexican food in the city.

The cactus salad and cochinita pibil are standout dishes, and the margaritas are not to be missed. Another great option is Pizzeria Bianco, a pizza place that has earned national acclaim for its wood-fired pies and fresh ingredients.

Phoenix is also home to a variety of international cuisines. Whether you're in the mood for sushi, Mediterranean, or even Ethiopian, you'll find plenty of options that will satisfy your cravings. For example, The Clever Koi offers a modern take on Asian comfort food.

When it comes to shopping, Phoenix offers a mix of high-end boutiques, local artisan markets, and vintage shops. If you're looking for unique souvenirs or handcrafted goods, check out the Melrose District, a trendy area filled with vintage shops and locally-owned stores. For a more upscale shopping experience, head to Scottsdale, just a short drive from Phoenix, where you'll find luxury retailers, art galleries, and fine dining.

No matter what type of food or shopping experience you're after, Phoenix has something to satisfy your appetite and your shopping needs. From farmer's markets to high-end malls, the city offers a mix of options that will make you want to come back for more.

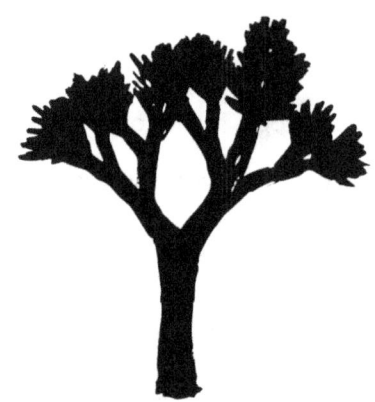

CHAPTER 4

Grand Canyon's North Rim and Beyond

"It's not the mountain we conquer, but ourselves."
—Sir Edmund Hillary

The Grand Canyon's North Rim is where solitude meets the sublime. Less crowded and more rugged than its southern counterpart, the North Rim offers a different perspective on this natural wonder. Here, you're not just gazing into the canyon—you're immersing yourself in its untamed beauty.

Off-the-Beaten-Path Trails at the North Rim

The North Rim is a hidden gem that feels like an entirely different world. Here, the crowds thin out, the air feels crisper, and the trails beckon you to explore their quiet majesty.

The North Rim boasts over 1,000 feet of additional elevation compared to the South Rim, which means cooler temperatures and lush forests of aspen and pine. You'll immediately notice the difference—it's wilder, more remote, and infused with a sense of adventure. A favorite trail on this side of the canyon is the Widforss Trail. Along the way, you'll traverse through dense forests and emerge onto ridges that reveal jaw-dropping canyon views.

Another trail you can't miss is the North Kaibab Trail. This one is unique because it's the only trail that takes you below the rim on this side of the canyon. It's a journey through time, with layers of rock formations telling a story that spans millions of years. You don't have to hike the entire trail to experience its magic. Even a short trek down to the Coconino Overlook gives you an unforgettable glimpse of the canyon's grandeur.

And the Ken Patrick Trail is a ticket to peace and quiet. This lesser-known path winds through a forest of ponderosa pines and opens up to sweeping vistas that make you feel like you're the only person on Earth. It's not uncommon to go hours without encountering another hiker, which is part of what makes this trail so special.

Discovering the Remote Beauty of Cape Royal

Cape Royal can steal your breath and make you feel like you've stepped into a postcard; this is it. The panoramic views here are unmatched, with the Colorado River snaking its way through the canyon far below. As the sun dips below the horizon during sunset, the canyon walls light up in shades of gold, pink, and orange.

One of the highlights of Cape Royal is the Angel's Window, a natural arch that frames the canyon beyond it. Walking out onto the viewing platform above Angels Window is a bit nerve-wracking if you're afraid of heights, but the view is worth conquering your fears.

Scenic Drives Through Kaibab National Forest

The journey through the Kaibab National Forest is nothing short of magical. As we leave the canyon's rim and head into the heart of the forest, you'll notice the landscape shift from arid desert to lush, green woodland. This is one of the few places where you can experience such dramatic contrasts in such a short distance.

The Forest Service Road 22 is a must-drive route. This gravel road takes us deep into the forest, where towering ponderosa pines stretch toward the sky. Along the way, we'll pass meadows that are often teeming with wildlife. Keep your eyes peeled—you might spot deer, wild turkeys, or even the elusive Kaibab squirrel, a species found only in this part of the world.

Another scenic drive you'll love is the Point Imperial Road. This paved route leads to the highest viewpoint on the North Rim, Point Imperial. From this vantage point, you can see the Painted Desert in the distance and the winding curves of the Colorado River far below. And because this area is less visited than other parts of the Grand Canyon, you often have the road to yourself.

Stargazing at the North Rim

When the sun sets on the North Rim, the adventure is far from over. This is when the stars come out to play, transforming the night sky into a celestial masterpiece. Thanks to the lack of light pollution, the North Rim is one of the best stargazing locations in the country.

A favorite stargazing spot is the Bright Angel Point. Here, you can lay back on the rocky outcrops and watch as the stars begin to twinkle above. On clear nights, you'll see constellations, shooting stars, and maybe even the faint glow of distant galaxies.

For a more immersive stargazing experience, consider joining one of the park's Ranger-led astronomy programs. These events are held regularly during the summer months and include telescope viewing and educational talks about the night sky. The rangers are incredibly knowledgeable, and their passion for the stars is contagious.

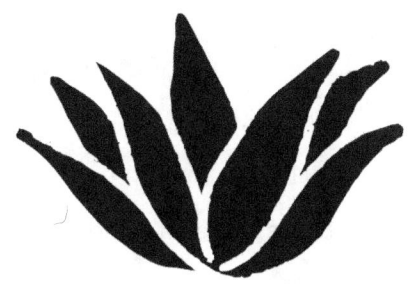

CHAPTER 5

Tucson and the Sonoran Desert

"The desert tells a different story every time one ventures on it."
–Robert Edison Fulton Jr.

Tucson is the kind of place where the spirit of the Southwest comes alive. Nestled in the heart of the Sonoran Desert, this vibrant city is surrounded by towering saguaro cacti, rugged mountains, and a unique blend of cultures that make it unlike anywhere else in the world.

Saguaro National Park and Desert Adventures

Let's kick things off with one of Tucson's crown jewels: Saguaro National Park. This park is split into two districts—east and west—flanking the city like a pair of protective arms. If you've never seen a saguaro cactus before, prepare to be amazed. These towering giants are the iconic symbols of the American Southwest, and they're even more impressive in person.

The Tucson Mountain District is home to some of the densest saguaro forests you'll ever see. The Valley View Overlook Trail is a great introduction. It's a relatively short hike, but it offers sweeping views of the desert floor dotted with saguaros as far as the eye can see. You'll want to come early or late in the day—the golden hour light transforms the desert into a photographer's dream.

For a more immersive experience, the Signal Hill Trail is a must. This easy hike leads to a hilltop adorned with ancient petroglyphs. Imagine standing in the same spot where indigenous peoples etched their stories into the rocks centuries ago. It's moments like these that make Saguaro National Park so special—it's not just a place of natural beauty but a living testament to history.

On the park's east side, the Rincon Mountain District, you'll find a different kind of magic. This area has higher elevations and more diverse vegetation, including oak and pine forests. The Cactus Forest Drive is a scenic loop that takes you through some of the most picturesque parts of the park.

You can pull over at various trailheads and overlooks to take it all in. If you're up for a longer hike, the Douglas Spring Trail offers an unforgettable journey into the Rincon Mountains, complete with seasonal waterfalls and breathtaking vistas.

Saguaro National Park is also a fantastic place for night adventures. The desert sky comes alive after dark, and stargazing here is second to none. If you're lucky, you might even catch a glimpse of nocturnal wildlife like owls, foxes, and coyotes. Trust me, there's nothing quite like hearing the howl of a coyote echoing through the stillness of the desert night.

The Best of Tucson's History and Culture

Tucson's rich history and vibrant culture are woven into every corner of the city. Walking through its streets, you'll find a blend of Spanish, Mexican, and Native American influences that give Tucson its unique character.

Starting at Mission San Xavier del Bac, often called the "White Dove of the Desert," this 18th-century Spanish mission is a masterpiece of Baroque architecture, and its gleaming white exterior against the blue desert sky is a sight to behold. As you step inside, you'll be greeted by intricate frescoes, ornate carvings, and a profound sense of tranquility.

Then head to El Presidio Historic District, the heart of Tucson's Old Town. As you wander through its narrow streets, you'll feel like you've stepped back in time. Some of the adobe buildings date back to the 19th century. Stop by the Tucson Museum of Art, which showcases an impressive collection of Southwestern art, from pre-Columbian artifacts to contemporary works.

Tucson is also home to a thriving food scene deeply rooted in its cultural heritage. Start with a visit to El Charro Café, the oldest Mexican restaurant in the U.S. that is still operated by the same family. Their carne seca, a dried beef dish made using traditional methods, is a must-try.

For a modern twist, head to Tucson Tamale Company, where you can sample tamales with fillings like green chile pork or black beans.

Art and culture enthusiasts should not miss the Tucson Folk Festival if you're visiting in the spring. This free, family-friendly event showcases live music, storytelling, and local crafts. It's a celebration of the region's artistic spirit and a great way to connect with locals.

Hiking Mount Lemmon and the Catalina Mountains

Next, head up to Mount Lemmon, the crown jewel of the Catalina Mountains. Rising over 9,000 feet above sea level, this mountain offers a refreshing escape from Tucson's scorching temperatures.

A favorite trail here is the Marshall Gulch Trail, a shaded path that winds through pine forests and alongside babbling brooks. The air here is cool and crisp, a stark contrast to the desert below. You'll pass wildflowers, towering trees, and the occasional rock formation that begs to be climbed. The trail connects to the Aspen Trail, creating a loop that offers stunning views of the surrounding mountains.

If you're up for a challenge, the Lemmon Rock Lookout Trail is a must. This steep, strenuous hike rewards you with panoramic views from the summit. On a clear day, you can see all the way to Mexico.

For those who prefer a more relaxed adventure, the SkyCenter Observatory offers guided nighttime stargazing programs. Mount Lemmon's high altitude and clear skies make it an ideal location for observing the stars.

Exploring the Arizona-Sonora Desert Museum

The Arizona-Sonora Desert Museum is part zoo, part botanical garden, and part natural history exhibit—all rolled into one incredible experience. If you want to truly understand the beauty and complexity of the Sonoran Desert, this is the place to start.

As you walk through the museum's outdoor exhibits, you'll encounter a stunning array of desert plants and animals. In the Riparian Corridor, you can see beavers, otters, and even a mountain lion in a recreated desert stream environment.

The Raptor Free Flight Program is another highlight. Watching these magnificent birds soar above you, responding to the calls of their trainers, is nothing short of magical. It's a rare chance to see hawks, falcons, and owls up close and learn about their role in the desert.

The museum also features an extensive cactus garden, showcasing everything from tiny barrel cacti to towering saguaros. Take your time here—you'll be amazed by the variety of shapes, sizes, and colors. The garden is especially beautiful in the spring when many of the cacti are in bloom.

For an educational experience, the museum's geology exhibit offers fascinating insights into the forces that shaped the Sonoran Desert. You can touch ancient rock formations, explore a recreated cave, and even learn about the region's mining history.

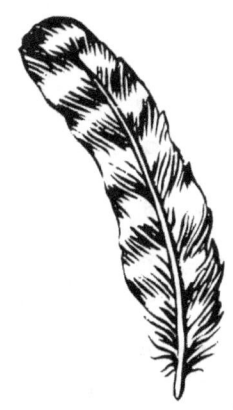

CHAPTER 6

The Wonders of Lake Powell and Page

"There is no greater beauty in the world than what we see in the places that we've never before."
—Anonymous

Nestled between the red rock formations of the Arizona-Utah border lies adventurers and nature lovers alike—Lake Powell. This reservoir stretches over 180 miles and offers stunning vistas, crystal-clear waters, world-renowned natural landmarks, and adrenaline-pumping outdoor activities.

Exploring the Glen Canyon Dam and Antelope Canyon

Page is the Glen Canyon Dam, a marvel of engineering that has shaped the landscape of Lake Powell. The dam stands tall, its impressive concrete walls towering 710 feet above the Colorado River. Built in the 1960s, the dam offers spectacular views and the chance to understand the history and significance of the area.

Next, let's explore Antelope Canyon, one of the most photographed and iconic slot canyons in the world. This natural wonder is located just outside of Page, and its unique rock formations make it a must-see. The narrow passageways of Antelope Canyon are carved into the Navajo Sandstone, with light filtering through the narrow slits, creating a play of shadows and warm colors that makes this place look almost surreal.

Antelope Canyon has two parts: Upper Antelope Canyon and Lower Antelope Canyon. Both are equally stunning, but they offer different experiences. Upper Antelope Canyon is more popular for photography and an easier hike.

Lower Antelope Canyon is a bit more adventurous. The narrow pathways and stairs make it a more physical experience, but the views are equally spectacular. Here, the walls of the canyon twist and turn in a way that makes it feel like you're walking through a natural cathedral of orange and red hues.

Boating, Kayaking, and Water Sports on Lake Powell

No trip to Lake Powell would be complete without experiencing the water firsthand. With over 1,900 miles of shoreline and crystal-clear water, the lake is a paradise for water lovers. Whether you're into boating, kayaking, or just cruising along in a houseboat, Lake Powell offers an endless variety of ways to explore.

If you're a fan of boating, you can explore secluded coves, navigate through narrow canyon walls, and even visit Rainbow Bridge, one of the world's largest natural rock arches.

For those who love to get a little more active on the water, kayaking is another fantastic option. Launch from Lone Rock Beach or any number of other convenient spots, and explore the coves and inlets at your own pace. Kayaking here allows you to get up close to the lake's stunning geology and gives you access to spots that larger boats can't reach.

If you're a fan of wakeboarding, water skiing, or paddleboarding, you'll find ample opportunities here as well. The waters are calm and smooth, perfect for catching air on a wakeboard or cruising the shoreline on a paddleboard.

Hiking and Photography in Horseshoe Bend

Just outside of Page, the Colorado River forms a perfect horseshoe shape, framed by steep red rock cliffs. It's a photographer's dream and a place that will take your breath away.

The Horseshoe Bend Trail is about a mile round-trip. The trail is well-marked and takes you across a sandy path to the edge of the cliff, where you'll be greeted with the awe-inspiring view of the river curving through the canyon below. The colors of the rock formations—ranging from deep reds to burnt oranges—contrast with the vibrant blue-green river.

If you're up for more hiking, there are also several nearby trails that offer great perspectives of the Colorado River and surrounding rock formations. The Kayenta Trail offers a longer, more strenuous hike and will lead you to more stunning views of the canyon, so if you want to take your exploration even further, this is a great option.

The Best Views and Hidden Gems Around Page

Page might be small, but it's surrounded by some of the most jaw-dropping landscapes in the Southwest, and it's packed with hidden gems just waiting to be explored.

The Wave is a stunning sandstone formation located in the Paria Canyon-Vermilion Cliffs Wilderness. The undulating waves of red, orange, and white rock make it look like something out of a dream, and the location is remote enough that it feels like a secret waiting to be discovered. It's a tough hike to reach, and you need a permit to access it, but the reward is absolutely worth it.

Waterholes Canyon is located outside of Page. This slot canyon is less crowded than Antelope Canyon, yet it's just as mesmerizing. The light inside the canyon creates beautiful shadows and highlights. Waterholes Canyon is the perfect place for those looking for a more serene and personal adventure.

For some incredible views, head to Castle Rock, which is visible from many parts of Lake Powell. It's a popular spot for photographs and offers fantastic views of the surrounding desert landscape. You can reach the base by boat, or if you're feeling adventurous, you can hike up the rocky slopes to capture some panoramic shots of the lake and the surrounding cliffs. Page is full of surprises, and the best way to uncover these gems is to venture off the beaten path.

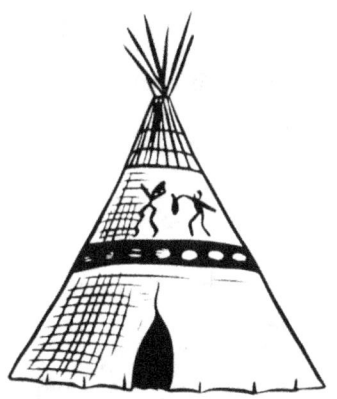

CHAPTER 7

Arizona's Native American Heritage and Cultural Sites

"To understand the true heart of a land, you must first understand the people who have lived in it for centuries."
—Anonymous

As you explore the vast landscapes of Arizona, you'll quickly discover that the land itself is more than just a canvas of desert plains, red rocks, and towering cacti. It is the living history of ancient civilizations that have called this place home for thousands of years.

Visiting the Hopi and Navajo Reservations

Arizona is home to two of the most prominent Native American tribes in the United States: the Hopi and the Navajo. Both tribes have deep-rooted traditions that go back centuries, and a visit to their reservations offers a rare opportunity to learn firsthand about their cultures, art, and way of life.

The Hopi Reservation, located in northeastern Arizona, is one of the oldest continuously inhabited places in the United States. The Hopi people are known for their deep spiritual connection to the land and their remarkable ability to live in harmony with nature. They are famous for their intricate Kachina dolls, pottery, and weaving, all of which hold profound cultural significance.

When you visit the Hopi Reservation, you'll have the chance to explore the Hopi Villages, some of which have been perched atop mesas for over a thousand years.

One of the most important experiences on the Hopi Reservation is a visit to the Hopi Cultural Center, where you can learn about the tribe's history, rituals, and art. The center also has a museum and gift shop where you can purchase authentic Hopi crafts, which help support the local community. If you time your visit right, you may even have the chance to witness a traditional Hopi dance ceremony or other sacred events that connect the Hopi people to their ancestors.

The Navajo Nation, covering over 27,000 square miles across northeastern Arizona, is the largest Native American reservation in the United States. The Navajo people are renowned for their rich cultural heritage, which includes weaving, jewelry-making, and traditional rug-making.

One of the highlights of a visit to the Navajo Reservation is the opportunity to tour the Monument Valley Navajo Tribal Park. The iconic sandstone formations that rise up from the desert floor.

You can take a guided tour with a Navajo guide, who will share insights into the history, culture, and spiritual significance of the land.

The Navajo Code Talkers Museum in Window Rock, the capital of the Navajo Nation, is another must-see. It honors the Navajo soldiers who played a crucial role in World War II by using their language to create an unbreakable code for military communications.

The Petrified Forest and Painted Desert

As you travel through northeastern Arizona, the Petrified Forest and the Painted Desert stand as a testament to the power of nature and time. Both are geological wonders with rich cultural history embedded in their very layers of rock.

Together, these two landscapes create one of the most visually striking places in Arizona, and they offer visitors a chance to explore both ancient natural history and the cultural heritage of the Native peoples who have lived in the area for centuries.

The Petrified Forest National Park is a mesmerizing landscape filled with colorful, fossilized trees that date back over 200 million years. These ancient trees, once part of a lush forest, were buried by volcanic ash and preserved as petrified wood. As you walk through the park, you'll see logs that have turned into stone, their vibrant colors ranging from shades of red and orange to purple and green.

The park has several well-marked trails, and the Blue Mesa trail is particularly striking. The blue and purple hues of the petrified wood contrast beautifully with the desert's red soil and skies.

Adjacent to the Petrified Forest is the Painted Desert, a stretch of land known for its stunning array of colors. The desert's mesas, buttes, and cliffs are painted in shades of red, orange, pink, and purple.

One of the best ways to experience the Painted Desert is by taking a drive along the Painted Desert Rim Drive. You'll be able to stop at various overlooks and trails, each offering a unique perspective of the desert's beauty. The Painted Desert has long been significant to Native American cultures. The landscape is woven into the creation myths of the Navajo and Hopi peoples, and it remains a place of deep spiritual significance.

The Heard Museum

If you want to delve deeper into Arizona's Native American heritage, a visit to the Heard Museum in Phoenix is essential. The museum is one of the most comprehensive and respected institutions for preserving and showcasing Native American art and culture.

The Heard Museum boasts an impressive collection of Native American art, ranging from traditional to contemporary pieces. You'll see intricate silver jewelry, pottery, textiles, and basketry, each representing different tribes and artistic traditions.

One of the highlights of the museum is its American Indian Hall, which houses an extensive collection of historic objects, including clothing, tools, and ceremonial items that tell the story of Native American life before European contact.

The museum's exhibits are designed not only to educate visitors but also to honor the vibrant cultures they represent. The Native Peoples of the Southwest exhibit is particularly insightful, as it showcases the diverse cultures of the region, including the Hopi, Navajo, and Zuni tribes, among others. The museum also regularly hosts temporary exhibitions that highlight contemporary Native American artists, offering a fresh perspective on the evolving landscape of Native American art.

One of the most powerful aspects of the Heard Museum is its focus on storytelling. Many of the exhibits are accompanied by personal stories from Native American artists and elders, allowing you to hear their voices and connect with the cultural significance of the pieces on display. The museum also hosts cultural events, including traditional dance performances, workshops, and lectures, providing a deeper understanding of Native American traditions.

Exploring the Ruins of Canyon de Chelly

Finally, no journey through Arizona's Native American heritage would be complete without a visit to the ruins of Canyon de Chelly. Located in northeastern Arizona, Canyon de Chelly is one of the most well-preserved archaeological sites. It's also one of the most spiritually significant places for the Navajo people.

The canyon is home to a number of ancient Ancestral Puebloan ruins, including cliff dwellings that date back to around 350 AD. The most famous of these is the White House Ruin, which is accessible via a short hike and offers a stunning view of the well-preserved dwellings nestled in the canyon's walls. Many of the ruins are still sacred sites for the Navajo people, and visitors are encouraged to approach the area with respect and reverence.

The Canyon de Chelly National Monument is located within the Navajo Nation, and it's a place where history, culture, and natural beauty come together in a truly unforgettable way. Whether you're exploring the cliff dwellings, admiring the sweeping vistas, or listening to the ancient stories of the Navajo people, Canyon de Chelly is a place that will stay with you long after you've left.

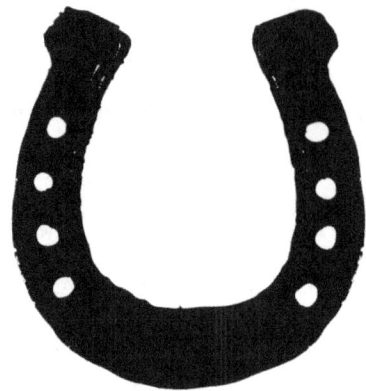

CHAPTER 8

Historic Route 66 and Arizona's Old West

"The great American road trip is about exploring the spirit of freedom, and no highway better embodies that spirit than Route 66."

Route 66 is not just a road; it's a legend, an iconic symbol of the American journey. In Arizona, the road cuts through some of the most captivating landscapes and historical sites in the country.

A Road Trip Along Historic Route 66

If you've ever dreamed of taking a road trip that feels like stepping into history, Arizona's stretch of Historic Route 66 is a must. A journey along this iconic highway is more than just a scenic drive; it's a true American adventure.

For many, Route 66 is known as "The Main Street of America," and it's easy to see why. This historic highway, which once spanned nearly 2,500 miles from Chicago to Santa Monica, is known for its charming towns, quirky roadside attractions, and scenic vistas it offers.

Arizona's section of Route 66 is a unique window into the past. Walking through small towns and past striking desert landscapes, you'll encounter everything from well-preserved motels and neon signs to historic gas stations and diners.

Let's explore most iconic stops along this historic road, beginning with three towns that epitomize the essen Selceigman, Williams, and Kingman.

Visiting Seligman, Williams, and Kingman

Let's start with Seligman, a small town that's become one of the most celebrated stops along Route 66. Nestled in the high desert, Seligman is like a time capsule, capturing the essence of the 1950s and 1960s roadside Americana. As you roll into town, you'll be greeted by an explosion of color and character: vintage gas stations, retro diners, and charming storefronts line the main street.

There's something magical about the way Seligman has preserved its Route 66 heritage. Many of the buildings still feature the original signs, offering an authentic look at what life was like for travelers during the highway's heyday.

One of the must-see stops in Seligman is the Snow Cap Drive-In, a quirky diner that's practically a legend in its own right. Established in the 1950s, the Snow Cap has become known for its colorful decor, playful atmosphere, and delicious burgers.

As you continue your road trip westward, Williams awaits you—a town that prides itself on being "The Gateway to the Grand Canyon." The town has made sure to preserve much of its historic charm, from the old-fashioned railroads to the historic hotels and motels lining the street. Williams is the place to experience a blend of Old West history and Route 66 nostalgia, with attractions like the Grand Canyon Railway. Williams hosts the annual "Route 66 Festival," a celebration of the highway's legacy, where visitors can enjoy classic cars, live music, and more.

Not far from Williams is Kingman. Kingman's Main Street is lined with motels, gas stations, and diners that hark back to the golden age of road trips. The Mohave Museum of History and Arts is also worth a visit, offering exhibits on the region's history, including its role as a key stop on Route 66.

<u>Exploring Arizona's Mining Towns</u>

As you continue your journey along Route 66, a detour through Arizona's mining towns is an absolute must. Two of the most fascinating towns you can visit are Jerome and Bisbee, both of which offer a deep dive into Arizona's industrial past.

Jerome, once known as the "Wickedest Town in the West," sits on the side of Cleopatra Hill, offering jaw-dropping views of the surrounding Verde Valley. This former copper mining town flourished in the early 20th century but faced economic decline after the mines were depleted. Today, Jerome has reinvented itself as an artist enclave, with galleries, shops, and restaurants occupying historic buildings that once housed miners and their families.

The Jerome State Historic Park is an essential stop in town, offering a fascinating look at the history of the area. Located in the former mansion of the local mine manager, the park houses exhibit the town's mining history and the people who lived and worked there.

Don't forget to stop by the Jerome Grand Hotel, a former hospital-turned-boutique hotel with a reputation for being one of the most haunted places in the state. Whether you're a history lover, a thrill-seeker, or simply someone who appreciates the beauty of a well-preserved historic town, Jerome will leave a lasting impression.

A short drive from Jerome is Bisbee, another former mining town. Known for its Victorian architecture and artistic atmosphere, Bisbee has become a haven for artists, musicians, and history buffs alike. The town's history as a copper mining hub is still evident, with the Queen Mine offering guided tours that take you deep into the earth to explore the tunnels where miners once worked.

Bisbee's preservation efforts have kept much of its 19th-century charm intact, making it a great place to soak up the Old West ambiance. A visit to Bisbee is a chance to explore both the past and present, as the town's rich history and artistic spirit blend seamlessly into the modern-day culture.

Arizona's Cowboy Heritage and Museums

No exploration of Arizona's Route 66 would be complete without delving into the state's cowboy heritage. Arizona's Wild West history is alive and well, with numerous museums and historical sites that celebrate the state's legacy of cattle ranching, lawmen, and outlaws. From gunfights to cattle drives, Arizona's cowboy heritage is woven into the fabric of its culture, and there are plenty of places where you can step into that world.

One of the most iconic places to learn about Arizona's cowboy past is the Arizona Cowboy Hall of Fame in Phoenix. This museum is dedicated to preserving the legacy of the men and women who shaped the state's Western culture. From rodeo champions to ranchers, the Hall of Fame honors those who contributed to Arizona's cowboy heritage, and it's a must-visit.

Another great stop is the Western Spirit: Scottsdale's Museum of the West. This museum showcases the history of the American West, with exhibits that highlight Native American culture, cowboy life, and the role of Arizona in shaping the West. The museum's collection includes artifacts, art, and interactive exhibits that offer a deep dive into the stories of the pioneers, settlers, and cowboys.

Next, Tombstone is a must-visit. Famous for the gunfight at the O.K. Corral, Tombstone has preserved much of its historic charm with reenactments and museums that bring the Wild West to life. From walking the streets where legends like Wyatt Earp and Doc Holliday once roamed to visiting the famous Bird Cage Theatre, Tombstone is a place where the past and present collide in a thrilling way.

Arizona's cowboy heritage is alive and well, and whether you're exploring a museum or taking in a reenactment, you'll find yourself immersed in the history of the Old West at every turn. From the preservation of historic towns like Jerome and Bisbee to the celebration of cowboy culture through museums and landmarks, Arizona offers a fascinating glimpse into the rugged, adventurous past of the American West.

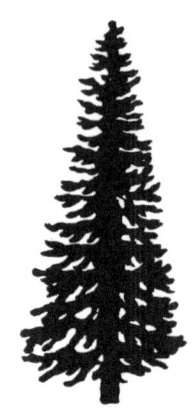

CHAPTER 9

Arizona's Outdoor Adventures for Thrill Seekers

"The best view comes after the hardest climb."
—Unknown

For thrill-seekers, Arizona is nothing short of an outdoor paradise. With its vast deserts, towering mountains, and rugged canyons, Arizona offers a plethora of adrenaline-pumping adventures that are sure to get your heart racing.

Whitewater Rafting on the Colorado River

There's something exhilarating about the combination of rushing water, towering canyon walls, and the raw power of nature that makes whitewater rafting on the Colorado River one of the most thrilling outdoor experiences in Arizona.

The Colorado River, winding its way through the Grand Canyon, is at the heart of Arizona's outdoor adventure scene. The river cuts through ancient rock formations, carving out the canyon that has become one of the Seven Natural Wonders of the World. The beauty of the canyon, combined with the adrenaline of navigating the river's rapids, creates an adventure like no other.

The most famous section of the river, the Grand Canyon, includes rapids ranging from class II to class V, with names like "Crystal" and "Hance" that will make your heart race as you approach them.

For those who want to make the most of their rafting experience, several outfitters in the area offer guided trips. These trips vary in length, ranging from half-day adventures to multi-day excursions. The guides are experts in navigating the river and offer fascinating insights into the geology, history, and wildlife of the Grand Canyon.

Rock Climbing in Arizona's Desert and Mountains

If you're looking for a challenge that will take you to new heights—literally—Arizona's desert and mountain landscapes are the perfect backdrop for rock climbing. From towering sandstone formations to jagged mountain peaks, Arizona is home to some of the best climbing spots in the country.

One of the most popular climbing destinations in Arizona is the town of Sedona. Known for its stunning red rock formations, Sedona offers a variety of climbing routes that cater to all skill levels. From the beginner-friendly climbs on Bell Rock to the more advanced challenges on Cathedral Rock, Sedona is a mecca for rock climbers.

The beauty of climbing in Sedona lies not just in the technical challenges but also in the awe-inspiring views that unfold as you ascend. The striking red rocks, balanced rocks, and vortex sites make Sedona one of the most visually stunning places to climb.

Further south, the Superstition Mountains offer another iconic climbing destination. Located just east of Phoenix, the Superstitions are home to dramatic, rugged cliffs and canyons, providing both technical rock climbing and bouldering opportunities.

The area is known for its challenging routes, especially around Weavers Needle, a distinctive rock spire that is a popular landmark for climbers. The rugged terrain of the Superstitions, combined with the remote nature of the area, makes climbing here an exciting adventure for experienced climbers.

For those who want to test their limits even further, the high-altitude climbs in the White Mountains are worth considering. Located in northeastern Arizona, the White Mountains are home to some of the state's tallest peaks. These climbs provide not only a physical challenge but also a mental one, as they require navigating through alpine terrain and dealing with the unpredictable weather conditions that come with high-altitude climbing.

Off-Roading and ATV Adventures

Arizona's rugged terrain is the perfect playground for off-roading enthusiasts. With vast deserts, towering mountains, and expansive forests, the state offers an unparalleled selection of off-road trails and ATV routes that will push your limits while allowing you to explore some of the most remote and scenic areas of the state.

One of the most famous off-roading destinations in Arizona is the area around Lake Pleasant, located just north of Phoenix. Here, you'll find an extensive network of trails that wind through rugged desert landscapes and provide a variety of terrain for off-road vehicles.

Further south, the Sonoran Desert offers a completely different off-roading experience. With its expansive sand dunes and cacti-studded landscapes, the desert is a playground for ATV and dirt bike enthusiasts. The Ironwood Forest National Monument, just west of Tucson, is home to a variety of off-road trails that cater to both beginners and experienced riders.

For those looking for more technical off-roading challenges, the Arizona Strip area near the Grand Canyon offers some of the state's most rugged and remote terrain. The trails in this region are often steep and rocky, requiring advanced skills and specialized vehicles. However, the rewards are well worth the effort, as you'll be able to experience some of the most stunning views in Arizona, including vistas of the Grand Canyon and the surrounding desert.

Horseback Riding Through Arizona's Scenic Trails

Horseback riding is one of the most immersive ways to experience Arizona's stunning landscapes. Arizona's wide-open spaces and scenic trails are ideal for equestrians of all skill levels, and the feeling of connecting with the land on horseback is a thrill in itself.

One of the best places to go horseback riding in Arizona is in the high desert of Sedona. Here, you can saddle up and ride through the red rock canyons and oak creek valleys, taking in views of the surrounding mesas and rock formations.

Sedona is known for its energy vortex sites, and many riding tours will take you to these unique locations, allowing you to connect with the land while on horseback. The trails here are diverse, ranging from easy, leisurely rides to more challenging routes that take you up into the hills for panoramic views.

For a truly Western experience, consider riding through the Arizona Sonora Desert, home to vast stretches of cactus forests and mountain landscapes. The Tanque Verde Ranch, located in the foothills of the Rincon Mountains near Tucson, offers guided horseback riding tours that take you through the heart of the Sonoran Desert.

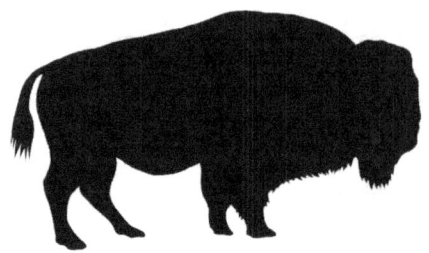

CHAPTER 10

Arizona's Best National and State Parks

"The earth has music for those who listen."
—George Santayana

Arizona's national and state parks are the epitome of outdoor adventure, offering iconic natural wonders and hidden gems that will captivate your spirit. With rugged deserts, vast canyons, towering pines, and ancient rock formations, these parks provide a landscape like no other.

A Complete Guide to Grand Canyon National Park

As one of the most visited national parks in the world, the Grand Canyon National Park offers endless opportunities for exploration, from hikes along the rim to thrilling descents into the canyon's depths.

The Grand Canyon is not just a geological marvel; it's a historical and cultural treasure. The park spans over 277 miles in length and reaches depths of over a mile, offering a jaw-dropping view of the Earth's history written in the layers of rock. But there's more to the canyon than meets the eye.

The Colorado River, which carved the canyon over millions of years, still flows through the heart of the park, providing opportunities for whitewater rafting and river adventures.

The most popular area of the park is the South Rim, easily accessible and home to the park's main visitor center. I recommend starting here, where you can take in breathtaking panoramic views and plan your exploration from several scenic overlooks.

The Bright Angel Trail and South Kaibab Trail are two of the most famous routes. Bright Angel Trail, with its stunning views and manageable distance, is great for those new to canyon hiking. However, keep in mind that hiking down into the canyon is one thing; hiking back up is another.

For those seeking a more relaxed experience, there are plenty of easy walks along the rim, such as the Rim Trail, which offers unobstructed views without the strenuous effort of descending into the canyon. Alternatively, consider riding the Grand Canyon Railway, a vintage train ride that takes you on a scenic journey from Williams to the park's South Rim. The Grand Canyon also offers some unique experiences, including stargazing at night. As a designated International Dark Sky Park, the Grand Canyon is one of the best places in the country to see the stars.

Visiting Petrified Forest National Park

Petrified Forest National Park is one of Arizona's hidden gems, a place where ancient history and striking natural beauty meet. This park is a world-renowned fossil site known for its colorful, petrified wood, which is millions of years old.

One of the best ways to experience the park is by taking a scenic drive along the park's main road, which passes by some of the most iconic features, including the Rainbow Forest and the Blue Mesa. As you wind your way through the park, you'll see the remarkable petrified logs, some of which are as large as trees and are brilliantly colored in shades of red, pink, purple, and yellow. These fossilized trees were once part of a lush forest long before the area became a desert. Over millions of years, the wood turned to stone, preserving the intricate patterns and textures of the original trees.

But Petrified Forest is more than just its petrified wood. The park also features ancient petroglyphs left by the Native American tribes who once lived in the region, as well as a fascinating collection of historic Route 66 landmarks. The Painted Desert Inn, a historic building originally built in the 1930s, is a great stop to learn about the park's history and the cultures that shaped it. The inn now serves as a museum and a visitor center where you can explore exhibits that bring the past to life.

For hikers, the park offers several trails that allow you to get up close to the petrified wood and explore the area on foot. The Crystal Forest Trail is one of the park's most popular, providing an easy stroll among the colorful logs. If you're looking for something more challenging, the Blue Mesa Trail takes you down into a canyon, where the scenery is nothing short of otherworldly.

The Petrified Forest is also a great place for stargazing, as it's located in a remote part of Arizona with little light pollution. If you're visiting during the summer months, the park hosts evening programs where you can learn about the night sky and the constellations visible from this unique location.

Exploring Slide Rock State Park and Oak Creek Canyon

Slide Rock State Park is the perfect blend of natural beauty and outdoor fun, especially if you're looking to cool off during the hot Arizona summers. Nestled in Oak Creek Canyon, this park offers one of the most unique swimming experiences in the state. The park's namesake is Slide Rock, a natural water slide created by smooth, red rock that allows you to slide down into the crystal-clear creek below.

The park is located just outside Sedona, a town famous for its striking red rock formations and vibrant arts scene. As you drive into the park, you'll be struck by the beauty of Oak Creek Canyon, a lush and narrow canyon surrounded by towering cliffs. The canyon is a haven for hikers, with several trails that offer views of the creek, waterfalls, and surrounding forests.

The Slide Rock area is great for families, as the water is shallow enough for children to play safely, while the surrounding rocks provide plenty of spots to relax and soak in the scenery.

The natural water slide is the main attraction, and it's easy to see why. The smooth, sloping rocks form a slippery slide that sends you careening down into the cool water below, providing both a refreshing and exhilarating experience. The park also features several other swimming holes where you can take a dip or simply relax by the water.

Aside from swimming, the park offers a range of activities, including hiking, picnicking, and wildlife watching. Oak Creek Canyon is home to various species of birds and other wildlife, making it a great spot for nature enthusiasts. The area is also known for its apple orchards, and in the fall, you can visit the park for apple picking, making it a perfect seasonal destination.

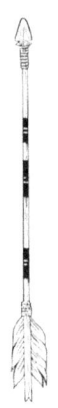

CHAPTER 11

Arizona Wine Country and Vineyards

"There is no wine like the one shared with a friend."
—Unknown

Arizona may not be the first place that comes to mind when you think of wine country, but the state is quickly becoming one of the most exciting destinations for wine lovers. From the lush valleys of Verde Valley to the sun-drenched hills of Willcox and Sonoita, Arizona's wine regions offer unique wines crafted from the state's diverse terroirs.

Willcox, Sonoita, and Verde Valley

When you think of wine, you might imagine rolling hills in California or the lush vineyards of Napa Valley. But Arizona's wine country is gaining ground, especially in three key regions: Willcox, Sonoita, and Verde Valley. Each of these areas offers a unique landscape and climate that has proven ideal for growing a variety of grapes.

The Willcox region, located in southeastern Arizona, is often referred to as the heart of the state's wine country. Its high elevation, combined with the warm days and cool nights, creates an ideal environment for growing grapes that yield rich and full-bodied wines. Willcox has a rich history of agriculture, and over the past few decades, it has become a hotspot for wine production.

The region's vineyards are relatively young, but they are producing some truly remarkable wines, particularly Syrah, Zinfandel, and Tempranillo. The Willcox wine region is a bit of a hidden gem, with small boutique wineries offering intimate tastings and an opportunity to meet the passionate winemakers behind the wines.

Traveling north to Sonoita, you'll encounter another unique wine-producing area. Sonoita is located in the southeastern part of Arizona, within the Santa Rita Mountains. The vineyards here benefit from the high-altitude climate, which offers warm days and cool evenings—perfect for growing Bordeaux-style grapes.

Sonoita's wine region is the oldest in the state, and it's also home to Arizona's first commercial vineyard, planted in the early 1980s. The region produces a variety of wines, from rich reds to crisp whites, and is especially known for its exceptional Pinot Noir and Malbec. Sonoita is smaller and less commercial than Willcox, but its scenic beauty and cozy tasting rooms make it a must-visit destination for anyone looking to experience Arizona wine country.

Lastly, we head north to the Verde Valley, which is considered Arizona's wine frontier. Located between the towns of Sedona and Cottonwood, the Verde Valley wine region has grown rapidly in recent years. It's situated at an elevation that allows the vines to grow in a climate that is perfect for developing complex, layered wines. The area is known for its diverse soils, which gives each vineyard its own distinct flavor profile.

The most popular varietals in the Verde Valley are Syrah, Merlot, and Chardonnay, though you'll also find excellent small-batch wineries producing unique blends. The Verde Valley is a fantastic place to explore, with wineries nestled alongside the region's dramatic red rock formations, offering a truly unforgettable experience for wine lovers.

The Best Arizona Vineyards to Visit and Tour

If you're planning a trip to Arizona's wine country, there are certain vineyards and wineries that should be at the top of your list.

In Willcox, one standout vineyard is the Kief-Joshua Vineyards. Known for its commitment to sustainable farming, Kief-Joshua offers tastings of its well-balanced wines, including its signature Syrah and Tempranillo.

Another must-visit in Willcox is Vigneron Winery, which has been garnering praise for its Rhone varietals and small-batch wines. The winery offers a cozy tasting room where you can sample their Syrah, Grenache, and other varieties while learning about the unique growing conditions in the Willcox region.

In Sonoita, the Arizona Stronghold Vineyards is a wine lover's paradise. Known for their exceptional quality, the vineyard's focus is on creating wines that reflect the local terroir. Their tasting room provides a welcoming atmosphere where you can try their highly-rated blends, such as the Chupacabra Red, a delicious combination of Syrah and Zinfandel.

Another gem in Sonoita is Callaghan Vineyards, which has been producing wines for more than 20 years. This family-owned winery specializes in wines that capture the essence of the Southern Arizona terroir. Their Sangiovese and Malbec are highly regarded, but their Café blend is what truly shines.

If you find yourself in the Verde Valley, Page Springs Cellars is a winery you simply can't miss. Nestled near the shores of Oak Creek, the vineyard boasts a stunning view of the surrounding landscape, making it a perfect spot to enjoy a glass of wine.

Their Tempranillo and Viognier are standouts, but their tasting room offers a selection of wines that range from bold reds to crisp whites. The vineyard's commitment to sustainable farming and natural winemaking methods adds a layer of authenticity to your visit, giving you a true taste of the Verde Valley.

For a more intimate experience, head to Pillsbury Wine Company, a small but mighty winery known for its meticulously crafted wines. Their Chardonnay and Grenache are particularly noteworthy, but their limited-edition releases are worth seeking out.

Pairing Wine with Arizona's Best Cuisine

Arizona's wine country isn't just about the wine—it's about the experience, and that includes pairing the state's best wines with its exceptional cuisine. Arizona's culinary scene has blossomed in recent years, with chefs creating dishes that are just as memorable as the wines produced in the state's vineyards.

When it comes to pairing wine with Arizona cuisine, start with the Sonoran-style dishes that are staples of the region. These flavorful meals, influenced by both Native American and Mexican traditions, often feature bold spices, chilies, and ingredients like corn, beans, and wild game.

A Tempranillo or Malbec from Sonoita pairs beautifully with dishes like carne asada, enchiladas, or barbecued pork. The richness and depth of the wine complement the smoky, spicy flavors of the meat, making for a balanced and satisfying experience.

For lighter fare, such as fresh seafood or grilled vegetables, consider pairing a crisp, dry Chardonnay or a refreshing Sauvignon Blanc from the Verde Valley. These wines, with their bright acidity and citrus notes, provide the perfect contrast to the fresh, clean flavors of dishes like grilled shrimp tacos or roasted corn salad.

If you're enjoying a hearty pasta or pizza dish, you can't go wrong with a Zinfandel or a Syrah from Willcox. These full-bodied reds have enough structure to stand up to rich, savory sauces and robust toppings like sausage, mushrooms, and aged cheese.

Wine Festivals and Tasting Events

One of the best ways to experience Arizona's wine culture is by attending one of the many wine festivals and tasting events held throughout the year.

The Arizona Wine Growers Association hosts the annual Arizona Wine Festival, which takes place in various locations across the state. This event features over 50 wineries from Willcox, Sonoita, Verde Valley, and other wine regions.

Another popular event is the Sonoita Wine & Art Festival, which celebrates the rich history of the Sonoita wine region. Held in May, this event draws wine lovers from across the country to taste wines from local wineries while enjoying live entertainment and local art.

And the Verde Valley Wine Festival is great. Held in the heart of Arizona's wine country, this festival showcases the best wines from the region's top wineries.

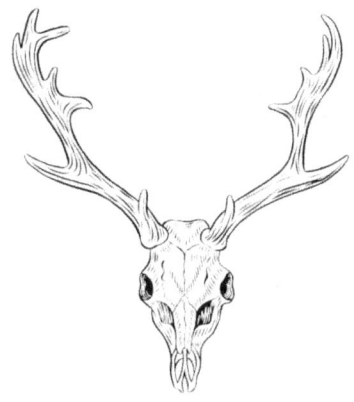

CHAPTER 12

Exploring the Arizona Tonto National Forest

"The forest is the best playmate, the natural wonder that invites us into a world where adventure and serenity dance together."
—Anonymous

Tonto National Forest is one of Arizona's crown jewels, an expansive and diverse wilderness that invites every type of adventurer. Stretching across nearly 3 million acres of pristine desert, riparian habitats, and rugged mountains, this national forest is a paradise for those seeking outdoor adventure.

Hiking the Scenic Trails of Tonto National Forest

Tonto National Forest is a hiker's dream. With over 200 miles of hiking trails, the forest offers some of the most scenic and diverse landscapes in Arizona. From easy strolls through desert washes to challenging climbs up jagged peaks, there's a trail suited to every level of hiker. And when I think about hiking in Tonto, I remember the crisp morning air, the scent of sagebrush on the breeze, and the majestic views that unfold at every turn.

One of the most iconic trails I've walked is the Saguaro Lake Trail, which offers panoramic views of Saguaro Lake and the surrounding desert landscape. The trailhead is located near the edge of the lake, and as you hike along, you'll find yourself marveling at the vastness of the desert—wide-open spaces dotted with cacti, dry riverbeds, and occasional bursts of color from blooming wildflowers.

It's an easy-to-moderate hike, making it perfect for families or those who want a leisurely stroll with a view.

For more experienced hikers, the Four Peaks Trail offers a much more challenging adventure. The trail leads you up to Four Peaks, one of the highest points in the forest. As you gain elevation, the landscape transforms from desert to ponderosa pine forests, and the air becomes cooler and fresher.

Another trail is the Peralta Trail near the Superstition Mountains. Known for its striking views of the Superstition Wilderness, this trail is one of the most popular in the forest. As you hike, you'll pass through diverse landscapes, including desert scrub and rocky outcrops. The trail ends at a viewpoint overlooking the Weaver's Needle, a towering rock formation that stands as a sentinel over the wilderness.

If you're looking for a more serene experience, the Tonto Creek Trail is a hidden gem. This trail takes you along the creek, where the sound of flowing water and the shade of tall cottonwoods create a peaceful atmosphere. The trail is relatively easy, with minimal elevation gain, making it perfect for a relaxing day hike. Along the way, you may spot wildlife, such as deer or birds.

Whether you're looking for an easy walk to clear your head or a strenuous challenge to push your limits, Tonto National Forest has a trail that's perfect for you. Each hike offers a unique way to explore the wilderness, with opportunities for solitude, exploration, and connection with nature.

Exploring Apache Lake and Roosevelt Lake

Apache Lake and Roosevelt Lake are two of Tonto National Forest's most tranquil spots. These lakes, nestled between rugged mountains and dry desert expanses, offer a refreshing escape from the heat and the perfect opportunity to connect with the water.

Apache Lake is the smaller of the two, but it's no less impressive. The lake is located along the Apache Trail, a historic route that traverses the eastern part of the forest.

The lake is somewhat remote, which makes it a great spot for those looking for a more peaceful experience away from the crowds. Boating, fishing, and kayaking are all popular activities here, and there's a certain tranquility that comes with spending a day on the water surrounded by mountains and deserts.

If you're an angler, Apache Lake offers some excellent fishing opportunities. The lake is stocked with various species of fish, including bass and catfish, and the surrounding area provides plenty of access points for both boaters and shore fishermen.

Roosevelt Lake, on the other hand, is the larger of the two lakes and is one of the most popular spots in Tonto National Forest. Located just off the Beeline Highway, Roosevelt Lake offers plenty of recreational opportunities, including boating, fishing, and watersports. The lake is surrounded by stunning desert and mountain scenery, with several marinas and boat ramps to choose from.

One of the highlights of Roosevelt Lake is the Roosevelt Lake Bridge, which spans the lake and offers some breathtaking views of the surrounding area. The bridge is particularly striking at sunset.

For those who enjoy boating, Roosevelt Lake offers ample space to explore, whether you're in a kayak, a canoe, or a motorized boat. The lake's many coves and inlets provide plenty of opportunities to find a quiet spot to relax, swim, or picnic. You can also rent a boat and spend the day exploring the lake or try your hand at water skiing or wakeboarding.

In addition to boating and fishing, both Apache Lake and Roosevelt Lake are great spots for hiking and camping. The areas surrounding the lakes offer several campsites.

The nearby trails, including those that loop around the lakes, provide opportunities for hiking, birdwatching, and photography, and the area is rich with wildlife.

Camping and Boating in Tonto National Forest

Camping and boating are two of the most popular activities in Tonto National Forest, and for good reason. The forest's vast landscape is dotted with countless campgrounds and secluded spots where you can set up camp and enjoy the great outdoors.

Some of the most popular campgrounds in Tonto include Blue Point Campground, located near Roosevelt Lake, and Tonto Creek Campground, nestled in the cool pine forests near the Mogollon Rim. These developed campgrounds offer amenities like picnic tables, fire rings, and restrooms, making them perfect for families and beginners.

For a more rustic experience, head to Fool Hollow Lake Recreation Area near Show Low. The area offers plenty of campsites set right on the water. It's a serene and peaceful spot.

Boating in Tonto National Forest is equally enjoyable, with several lakes offering opportunities for motorized boating, kayaking, canoeing, and paddleboarding. Roosevelt Lake, as mentioned earlier, is the largest and most well-known spot for boating in the forest, but there are other lakes that are equally beautiful and less crowded, such as Bartlett Lake and Horseshoe Reservoir. These lakes provide plenty of space to explore, and many offer boat rentals for those who don't have their own.

Whether you're kayaking along the shores of Saguaro Lake, cruising across the sparkling waters of Roosevelt Lake, or fishing from a boat on Apache Lake, the water activities in Tonto are nothing short of exhilarating.

Tonto National Forest also offers several backcountry camping opportunities where you can truly get away from it all and experience the wilderness in its rawest form. These primitive campsites require a bit more preparation and a willingness to disconnect from modern amenities. Just remember to follow Leave No Trace principles and pack out everything you bring in.

Wildlife Watching in the Tonto Wilderness

Wildlife watching in Tonto National Forest is an incredible experience. The forest is home to a rich diversity of animals, from desert-dwelling reptiles to majestic birds of prey and elusive mammals. Tonto National Forest offers a range of habitats, from desert and riparian areas to pine forests and rugged mountains, each attracting different species of wildlife.

One of the most iconic animals you'll encounter in Tonto is the desert bighorn sheep. These impressive creatures are well adapted to the harsh desert environment, and spotting them on the cliffs and hillsides is always a thrill.

Tonto is also home to a variety of bird species, making it a fantastic destination for birdwatching. The forest's diverse ecosystems attract everything from soaring eagles and red-tailed hawks to migratory songbirds and waterfowl. If you're a bird enthusiast, Tonto National Forest offers countless opportunities to spot these fascinating creatures in their natural habitats.

Of course, Tonto is also home to a variety of other animals, including coyotes, mountain lions, javelinas, and numerous species of snakes and lizards. While encounters with these creatures are rare, it's not unusual to hear the distant howls of a coyote or catch a fleeting glimpse of a mountain lion's tail disappearing into the brush. The forest is alive with activity, and every day spent in the wilderness offers the chance to spot something new and exciting.

In addition to wildlife viewing, Tonto National Forest is a great place to explore the plant life that supports this vibrant ecosystem. The forest is home to a wide variety of cacti, succulents, wildflowers, and trees, all of which provide essential food and shelter for the wildlife.

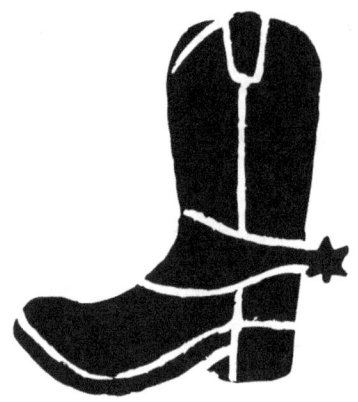

CHAPTER 13

The Wild West of Arizona: Tombstone and Bisbee

"The West was a land of limitless opportunity and untamed freedom, where legends were born and stories lived forever."

When you think of the Wild West, your mind likely conjures up images of dusty streets, dueling cowboys, and bustling saloons. Arizona, with its rich frontier history, is a treasure trove for anyone eager to explore this fascinating chapter of American history.

Walking Through Tombstone

Allen Street in Tombstone feels like stepping into a time machine. Here, the Old West isn't just a memory; it's alive and thriving. Tombstone calls itself "The Town Too Tough to Die."

The town's history began in 1877 when Ed Schieffelin, a prospector, was warned that he'd find his tombstone before he'd find silver. Instead, he struck it rich, naming the area Tombstone, and soon, the town became a bustling mining hub. Today, the charm of Tombstone lies in its authenticity. It hasn't been gentrified or polished; it's as rugged and rowdy as it was in the 19th century.

Start your journey with a stroll down Allen Street, the heart of Tombstone. This historic thoroughfare is lined with saloons, shops, and old-time photo studios where you can pose as a gunslinger or a saloon girl. Don't miss the Bird Cage Theatre, a place steeped in scandal and intrigue. This infamous saloon and brothel operated 24/7 in its heyday, and it is now a museum.

For a dose of local flavor, catch one of the live reenactments of the Gunfight at the OK Corral. The actors bring the legendary shootout to life with impressive detail, making you feel like you've been transported back to October 26, 1881.

Tombstone's charm lies not only in its history but also in its people. Their passion for preserving Tombstone's legacy is infectious, making your visit feel like more than just a history lesson—it's an experience.

History of the Gunfight at the OK Corral

No visit to Tombstone would be complete without delving into the infamous Gunfight at the OK Corral. This event wasn't just a random shootout; it was the culmination of simmering tensions between lawmen and outlaws, epitomizing the chaos of the Wild West.

To set the stage, the year was 1881. Tombstone was a booming town, attracting miners, gamblers, and outlaws in equal measure. Lawmen Wyatt Earp, his brothers Virgil and Morgan, and their friend Doc Holliday found themselves at odds with a group of cowboys known for cattle rustling and lawlessness. The conflict came to a head when the two factions met near the OK Corral.

The gunfight lasted only 30 seconds, but those fleeting moments have become immortalized in American folklore. Tombstone's meticulous preservation of this history allows visitors to relive the drama, whether through the reenactments or the detailed exhibits at the OK Corral Museum.

What's fascinating is how this event has been mythologized over the years. Hollywood has portrayed it as a classic tale of good versus evil, but the reality is far more complex. The Earps and their allies were no saints, and the cowboys were more than just villains. It's this nuanced history that makes the story so compelling.

Exploring Bisbee's Art Scene and Mining History

A short drive from Tombstone, Bisbee offers a striking contrast to the rugged frontier atmosphere. Known for its rich mining history and vibrant arts scene, this quirky town nestled in the Mule Mountains is a feast for the senses.

Bisbee began as a mining town in the late 19th century, producing staggering amounts of copper, gold, and silver. Today, the town has reinvented itself as a haven for artists, creatives, and anyone seeking an offbeat retreat. Walking through Bisbee, you'll notice how its mining roots and artistic evolution blend seamlessly.

Start your journey through Bisbee at the Queen Mine Tour. Guided by retired miners, the tour offers a fascinating glimpse into the lives of those who worked in the mines. Their stories are equal parts harrowing and inspiring, painting a vivid picture of Bisbee's past.

In Bisbee's arts district, the streets are lined with galleries, boutique shops, and murals that reflect the town's creative spirit. A favorite stop is the Bisbee Mining and Historical Museum, a Smithsonian affiliate that brilliantly captures the town's transformation from a mining hub to an artistic enclave.

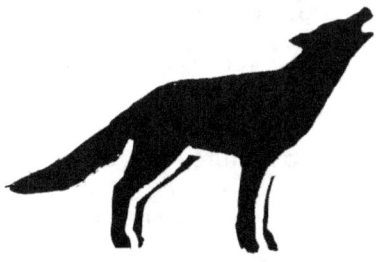

CHAPTER 14

Arizona's Hidden Gems and Lesser-Known Treasures

"The world is full of magical things, patiently waiting for our senses to grow sharper."
—W.B. Yeats

Arizona may be famous for its iconic landmarks like the Grand Canyon and Monument Valley, but some of the most rewarding experiences in the state come from discovering its hidden gems. These lesser-known treasures are where the soul of Arizona truly shines.

Exploring Arizona's Caves and Natural Formations

Caves have always held an air of mystery, and Arizona is home to a network of hidden caverns that feel like portals to another world. For example, Lava River Cave in Flagstaff is a mile-long lava tube that was formed around 700,000 years ago, and walking through it is like journeying into the Earth's core.

Another remarkable spot is Colossal Cave Mountain Park near Tucson. This dry cave system, used for centuries by Native Americans, is a treasure trove of history and geology. The guided tour takes you through chambers adorned with stalactites, stalagmites, and flowstone formations. The stories of bandits hiding loot in the cave added an extra layer of intrigue.

For those of you who love a bit of adventure, Kartchner Caverns State Park is a must-visit. Discovered in 1974 but kept secret for over a decade, this "living cave" is still growing its formations. The delicate formations, like soda straws and bacon ribbons, are a testament to the power of water and time. The park's dedication to preserving the cave's pristine condition makes it a truly special experience.

Hidden Hot Springs and Secluded Escapes

There's something deeply restorative about soaking in a natural hot spring, especially when it's tucked away in a serene, untouched setting. Arizona is blessed with several of these hidden oases, perfect for unwinding and reconnecting with nature.

For example, Castle Hot Springs is located in a secluded valley northwest of Phoenix. This historic resort, once frequented by the Rockefellers and Roosevelts, has been restored to offer a luxurious escape. The spring-fed pools are rich in minerals and surrounded by desert beauty, creating an idyllic atmosphere for relaxation.

If you're looking for something more rustic, the Verde Hot Springs near Camp Verde is a hidden gem with a fascinating history. Accessible only by a hike and a river crossing, these hot springs are remnants of a once-grand resort that burned down in the 1960s.

For a truly off-the-grid adventure, go to Sheep Bridge Hot Springs. Located in the rugged Tonto National Forest, these springs require a challenging drive and a short hike to reach. The effort is well worth it. The springs are nestled along the Verde River, offering stunning views of the surrounding wilderness.

Unique Local Attractions

In Bisbee, the Shady Dell offers a retro escape like no other. This vintage trailer park allows you to stay in restored Airstreams and Spartan trailers, each lovingly decorated to reflect the charm of the 1940s and 50s. It's like stepping back in time, complete with a retro diner for a nostalgic meal.

Another hidden treasure is the Mystery Castle in Phoenix, a quirky structure built in the 1930s by Boyce Gulley for his daughter. Constructed from salvaged materials, the castle is a whimsical maze of rooms, turrets, and oddities, each with its own story. Touring this eccentric home is a fascinating glimpse into the creativity and love that went into its creation.

Tonto Natural Bridge State Park is a hidden gem near Pine and is home to the world's largest natural travertine bridge. Hiking down to the bridge, with its cascading waterfalls and lush greenery, felt like entering a hidden paradise.

Arizona's Quirky Roadside Stops

No road trip through Arizona is complete without stopping at some of its quirky roadside attractions. These oddball destinations lead you through the state's rich and often bizarre history.

The Wigwam Motel in Holbrook is a Route 66 icon, with its teepee-shaped rooms that transport you back to the golden age of road trips. Staying here is like living in a postcard from the 1950s, complete with vintage cars parked outside each wigwam.

On another stretch of Route 66, you'll find the quirky town of Seligman, the inspiration for the Pixar movie Cars. This tiny town is a celebration of roadside Americana, with retro diners, souvenir shops, and colorful murals paying homage to its heritage.

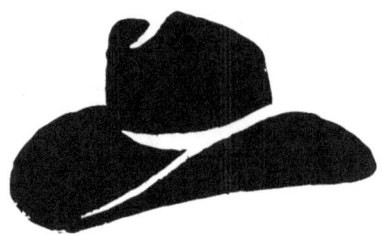

CHAPTER 15

Arizona for Family Adventures

"Family is not an important thing. It's everything."
—Michael J. Fox

Traveling with your family creates lifelong memories, and Arizona is a treasure trove of experiences that appeal to kids, parents, and even grandparents. Whether it's hiking trails where little ones can safely explore, interactive museums that engage curious minds, or resorts that make relaxation fun for everyone, Arizona offers something for every family dynamic.

Family-Friendly Hiking Trails and Outdoor Activities

Arizona's landscape is a playground for all ages, and hiking is one of the best ways to experience it together as a family. But not every trail is suited for young hikers.

Wind Cave Trail in Usery Mountain Regional Park is a 3-mile round-trip hike that is perfect for families, with a gradual incline and stunning desert views. At the trail's end, you're rewarded with a natural alcove that kids will love to explore.

For a bit more adventure, the easy trail around Watson Lake in Prescott is a gem. The granite boulders surrounding the lake provide endless opportunities for climbing, exploring, and taking Instagram-worthy family photos.

Don't overlook Sedona's Red Rock State Park, where the trails are short, flat, and scenic. The Eagle's Nest Loop offers breathtaking views, while the family-oriented nature center hosts interactive programs that teach kids about local wildlife.

For families with older children, kayaking on the Verde River is an unforgettable experience. The calm waters and occasional rapids make it exciting yet safe for beginners.

Arizona's outdoor adventures go beyond hiking. Consider a trip to Bearizona in Williams, where your family can drive through a wildlife park and see bears, wolves, and bison up close.

Outdoor activities like these help families connect with nature and each other. Watching your child marvel at a cactus or spot their first roadrunner is a reminder of the simple joys that make travel so meaningful.

Kid-Friendly Attractions and Museums in Arizona

While Arizona's natural wonders are hard to beat, its museums and attractions are just as captivating, especially for curious young minds. These kid-friendly spots combine education with fun, making them perfect for family visits.

The Arizona Science Center in Phoenix is an absolute must. From the hands-on exhibits to the planetarium shows, this museum is a playground for curious kids.

The Pima Air & Space Museum in Tucson is a sprawling complex that features over 400 aircraft, including a retired Air Force One.

The Dinosaur Tracks near Tuba City are an outdoor museum of sorts, where real fossilized tracks lie preserved in the desert rock. Local Navajo guides share fascinating stories about these prehistoric creatures, making it a fun and educational stop.

If your family loves animals, the Reid Park Zoo in Tucson is an intimate zoo with well-designed exhibits that bring you closer to the animals. The giraffe-feeding experience is always a hit.

A unique attraction is the Lowell Observatory in Flagstaff. Stargazing through powerful telescopes and learning about constellations is an awe-inspiring experience for kids and adults alike. On a clear night, the Milky Way seems close enough to touch.

CHAPTER 16

Arizona's Best Lakes and Water Activities

"Adopt the pace of nature: her secret is patience."
—Ralph Waldo Emerson

When most people think of Arizona, they imagine arid deserts and towering cacti. But Arizona is also a haven for water lovers. With its glittering lakes and riverfront escapes, the state offers countless opportunities to cool off, unwind, and reconnect with nature.

Lake Havasu and the London Bridge

Lake Havasu, a desert oasis straddling the Arizona-California border, is a destination that never fails to amaze me. What sets this lake apart isn't just its crystal-clear waters or its array of activities—it's the unexpected presence of the historic London Bridge. Yes, you read that right: the same bridge that once spanned the River Thames in England now resides in this lakeside town.

Let's start with the bridge itself. Transported piece by piece from London in the 1960s, the bridge is more than a quirky attraction; it's a testament to engineering and a fascinating piece of history.

Of course, Lake Havasu isn't just about the bridge. It's a hub for water sports, drawing in boaters, jet skiers, and paddleboarders from across the country. If you're into adrenaline-pumping activities, renting a jet ski is a fantastic way to explore the lake.

Fishing is a popular pastime here. The lake is teeming with bass, catfish, and bluegill, making it a haven for anglers of all skill levels.

If you're traveling with family, don't miss Rotary Community Park. With its sandy beach, shaded picnic areas, and playground, it's the perfect spot for a relaxing day by the water.

For a unique experience, consider booking a sunset cruise. As the sun dips below the horizon, the lake transforms into a shimmering canvas of gold and orange, creating a magical backdrop for your evening.

Boating, Fishing, and Water Sports on Lake Powell

Lake Powell, nestled within the Glen Canyon National Recreation Area, is more than just a lake—it's a labyrinth of canyons, caves, and waterways that seem almost otherworldly.

Boating is the crown jewel of activities at Lake Powell. Renting a houseboat is the ultimate way to explore this aquatic wonderland. Imagine waking up to the sound of gentle waves lapping against the boat, with towering red cliffs reflected in the water. That's Lake Powell for you.

If you're looking for something more fast-paced, the lake is a paradise for jet skiing, wakeboarding, and tubing.

Fishing enthusiasts will also find plenty to love at Lake Powell. The lake is home to an abundance of striped bass, walleye, and crappie.

But Lake Powell isn't just about the water. The surrounding area offers endless opportunities for exploration. A favorite experience is hiking to Rainbow Bridge National Monument, one of the largest natural bridges in the world. Accessible by boat and a short hike, this awe-inspiring formation is a must-see.

Whether you're seeking adventure, solitude, or simply a chance to marvel at nature's beauty, Lake Powell delivers on all fronts.

Exploring the Waters of Roosevelt and Apache Lakes

Nestled in the heart of Tonto National Forest, Roosevelt and Apache Lakes are two of Arizona's best-kept secrets. Unlike the more crowded Lake Havasu and Lake Powell, these lakes offer a quieter, more serene escape that feels like stepping back in time.

Roosevelt Lake, the largest lake entirely within Arizona, is a haven for anglers. The bass fishing here is legendary. The lake's calm surface and picturesque surroundings make it an ideal spot for kayaking and paddleboarding, too.

Apache Lake, with its steep canyon walls and crystal-clear waters, is equally enchanting. The drive to Apache Lake via the Apache Trail is an adventure in itself, with hairpin turns and breathtaking views that will leave you in awe. Once you arrive, you'll find a peaceful retreat perfect for boating, swimming, and simply soaking in the beauty of the desert landscape.

Roosevelt and Apache Lakes may not have the fame of their larger counterparts, but their unspoiled beauty and tranquil atmosphere make them true hidden gems.

Arizona's Best Beach and Lakefront Resorts

When you think of Arizona, beaches might not be the first thing that comes to mind. But the state's lakefront resorts offer sandy shores, luxurious amenities, and unforgettable experiences that rival any coastal destination.

Lake Havasu's Nautical Beachfront Resort is a standout, with its private beach, water sports rentals, and family-friendly atmosphere.

Lake Powell Resorts and Marinas is another excellent choice, especially for those planning to explore the lake by boat. With its comfortable accommodations, on-site dining, and proximity to Rainbow Bridge, it's the perfect base for a Lake Powell adventure.

If you're looking for a more rustic retreat, the Apache Lake Marina and Resort offers cozy cabins and a relaxed atmosphere.

CHAPTER 17

Arizona's Dark Skies and Stargazing Spots

"The stars don't look bigger, but they do look brighter from here."
—Sally Ride

In Arizona, the night skies here are like no other. Arizona is a haven for stargazers, offering some of the clearest and most stunning night skies in the world.

The Best Stargazing Locations in Arizona

If you're looking for the ultimate stargazing experience, Arizona has plenty to offer. A favorite spot is Kitt Peak National Observatory, located about an hour southwest of Tucson. Perched atop a mountain at 6,880 feet, Kitt Peak is home to one of the largest collections of telescopes in the world. Guided tours and nighttime programs make it a must-visit for both beginners and seasoned astronomers.

Another gem is Lowell Observatory in Flagstaff. This historic site is where Pluto was discovered in 1930, and its connection to astronomical history adds an extra layer of magic to any visit. On a clear night, the observatory's advanced telescopes allow you to see details of distant galaxies and nebulae that are otherwise invisible to the naked eye.

For those who prefer a more remote experience, Chiricahua National Monument is an excellent choice. Nestled in southeastern Arizona, this park's rugged terrain and minimal light pollution make it a stargazer's paradise.

Then there's Grand Canyon National Park, which offers breathtaking views both day and night. During the annual Grand Canyon Star Party, amateur and professional astronomers gather to share their knowledge and telescopes with visitors.

Arizona's deserts also have their own unique charm. Saguaro National Park, with its towering cacti silhouetted against a starry backdrop, offers a dramatic setting for stargazing. The silence of the desert night amplifies the beauty of the cosmos, making it an ideal spot for reflection and connection with nature.

Tips for Planning Your Arizona Stargazing Trip

Timing is everything. The best stargazing conditions occur during a new moon when the sky is at its darkest. Use a lunar calendar to plan your trip around this phase, and check the weather forecast for clear skies. Location is just as important. While Arizona's urban areas are beautiful, their light pollution can hinder your ability to see faint stars and celestial objects. Aim for remote locations like national parks, observatories, or dark sky parks. Apps like Dark Sky Finder can help you pinpoint areas with minimal light interference.

Arizona's Dark Sky Communities and Parks

Arizona is a leader in the dark sky movement, with several communities and parks dedicated to preserving the night sky for future generations. Visiting these places is not only a treat for stargazers but also a way to support efforts to combat light pollution.

One of the most notable dark sky communities is Flagstaff, the world's first International Dark Sky City. Here, you'll find a commitment to protecting the night sky that's evident in the city's lighting ordinances and public outreach programs. Flagstaff's residents take pride in their starry skies, and it shows.

Another standout is Sedona, known for its stunning red rock landscapes and equally breathtaking night skies. The city's strict lighting codes ensure that visitors can enjoy an unobstructed view of the stars.

Arizona is also home to numerous dark sky parks, including Kartchner Caverns State Park and Oracle State Park. These parks offer designated stargazing areas, educational programs, and even overnight camping options.

Celestial Events and Astronomy Festivals

One of the most exciting aspects of stargazing in Arizona is the opportunity to witness celestial events and attend astronomy festivals. From meteor showers to eclipses, there's always something happening in the sky.

The Perseid meteor shower, which peaks in August, is one of the most spectacular events of the year. With dozens of meteors streaking across the sky every hour, it's a sight that never fails to inspire awe.

Another must-see event is a total lunar eclipse. During these rare occurrences, the moon takes on a reddish hue, earning it the nickname "blood moon." Watching this phenomenon from the Arizona desert is an otherworldly experience that you won't want to miss.

Arizona also hosts several astronomy festivals, including the Grand Canyon Star Party and the Arizona Science and Astronomy Expo. These events bring together astronomy enthusiasts of all ages for telescope viewings, workshops, and guest lectures.

CHAPTER 18

Planning Your Arizona Road Trip

"The journey is the destination."
—Dan Eldon

There's something magical about a road trip—the open road, the freedom to stop wherever you like, and the thrill of discovering new places. With its breathtaking landscapes, vibrant cities, and hidden gems, Arizona is the perfect destination for an unforgettable road trip.

How to Plan Your Ultimate Arizona Road Trip

Planning an Arizona road trip is like preparing a masterpiece: it requires inspiration, strategy, and a willingness to embrace spontaneity.

Start by asking yourself what kind of road trip experience you want. Maybe you're craving a mix of both. Arizona offers everything from dramatic deserts to lush pine forests, so the key is to align your itinerary with your interests and the time you have.

Next, map out a rough route. While it's tempting to plan every detail, leave room for flexibility—you never know when you'll stumble upon a charming roadside café or an unmarked trail leading to a stunning vista. A good starting point is Phoenix, Arizona's bustling capital, which is conveniently located near major highways and offers plenty of attractions to kick off your journey. Consider a clockwise route through the state, hitting must-see spots like Sedona, Flagstaff, the Grand Canyon, Monument Valley, and Tucson.

One of the best ways to make the most of your trip is by prioritizing stops that showcase Arizona's diverse landscapes. You might begin with the Sonoran Desert, known for its towering saguaro cacti, before heading north to the red rocks of Sedona. From there, continue to the high-altitude pine forests of Flagstaff and the awe-inspiring Grand Canyon. Don't forget to include some lesser-known destinations like the Petrified Forest National Park or the quirky town of Bisbee.

When planning your accommodations, consider a mix of options. Arizona has everything from luxurious resorts and charming bed-and-breakfasts to campgrounds and RV parks.

Planning your ultimate Arizona road trip is an exciting process that sets the stage for an adventure you'll remember forever. Trust me, the effort you put into preparation will pay off when exploring the wonders of the Grand Canyon State.

Essential Stops and Hidden Gems Along the Way

Regarding Arizona road trips, the well-known landmarks are just the beginning. Sure, the Grand Canyon, Sedona, and Monument Valley deserve their fame, but a wealth of hidden gems is waiting to be discovered along the way.

Let's start with Antelope Canyon, a slot canyon near Page that looks like something out of a dream. Its swirling sandstone walls are illuminated by beams of sunlight, creating a surreal, almost otherworldly atmosphere. The canyon is a photographer's paradise, but standing inside this natural wonder is an unforgettable experience, even if you're not into photography.

Just a short drive from Antelope Canyon is Horseshoe Bend, a stunning overlook of the Colorado River. The view is so dramatic that it feels like Mother Nature sculpted it for a postcard.

To taste Arizona's history, stop in Jerome, a former mining town turned artist community. Perched on a mountainside, this quirky town has galleries, unique shops, and even a haunted hotel. Strolling through Jerome's narrow streets, you'll feel like you've returned in time.

Canyon de Chelly National Monument is in northeastern Arizona. It is home to ancient cliff dwellings and dramatic sandstone formations. Unlike the Grand Canyon, Canyon de Chelly is still inhabited by the Navajo people, adding a layer of cultural significance to its natural beauty.

Another must-see is Kartchner Caverns State Park, an incredible underground cave system near Benson. The caverns are living caves, meaning their formations are still growing, and the guided tours here are both educational and awe-inspiring.

As you explore these stops, look for roadside treasures. Arizona has quirky attractions like the London Bridge in Lake Havasu City, the Wigwam Motel on Route 66, and the Goldfield Ghost Town near Apache Junction. Each adds a dash of charm and character to your road trip.

Navigating Arizona's Scenic Byways

Arizona's scenic byways are more than just roads—they're gateways to some of the state's most breathtaking landscapes. From winding mountain passes to open desert highways, these routes are a joy to explore and offer opportunities to stop and soak in the views.

One of the most famous byways is State Route 89A, which runs from Prescott to Flagstaff. This route takes you through Sedona's stunning red rock country and Oak Creek Canyon, a lush, forested area that feels like an oasis in the desert.

Another must-drive is the Apache Trail, a historic route that winds through the Superstition Mountains and past Canyon Lake. The road is unpaved in some sections, which adds a sense of adventure, but the views of rugged cliffs and sparkling water are well worth it.

For a taste of Arizona's Wild West, take a drive along Historic Route 66. This iconic highway passes through charming towns like Williams, Kingman, and Winslow, where you can "stand on a corner," as the Eagles famously sang. Each town is filled with nostalgia and Americana, making it a fun and nostalgic experience.

If you want solitude and stunning desert vistas, head to the Ajo Scenic Loop in southern Arizona. This remote route takes you through Organ Pipe Cactus National Monument, where you'll find towering cacti and dramatic desert landscapes. It's a great place to connect with nature and enjoy peace.

CONCLUSION

"We travel not to escape life, but for life not to escape us."
–Anonymous

Arizona is a reminder of how vast and diverse our world is. Its deserts, mountains, and canyons are a testament to the power of nature, while its towns and cities showcase the creativity and resilience of the people who call this state home. By exploring Arizona, you've become a part of its story, and it has become a part of yours.

Bonus

Top 100 Bucket List Places to Visit in Arizona

Arizona isn't just a state; it's a living masterpiece—a symphony of colors, landscapes, and history waiting to be explored. This list combines adventure, inspiration, and the beauty of discovery, from majestic canyons to cultural treasures. Whether you're a thrill-seeker, a history buff, or someone chasing breathtaking views, these 100 destinations should inspire you to pack your bags and reconnect with awe.

Must-See Natural Wonders

1. **Grand Canyon National Park**—Stand in awe of one of the World's Seven Natural Wonders.

2. **Antelope Canyon**—Walkthrough sandstone slot canyons sculpted by time and water.

3. **Horseshoe Bend**—Witness the dramatic curve of the Colorado River from above.

4. **Petrified Forest National Park**—Explore ancient trees that have turned into stunning, multicolored stone.

5. **Sedona's Red Rock Formations**—Be mesmerized by crimson landscapes that have inspired generations.

6. **Monument Valley**—Iconic vistas that have graced countless films and postcards.

7. **Havasu Falls**—Discover turquoise cascades hidden deep within the Grand Canyon.

8. **The Wave**—Marvel at surreal sandstone waves (requires a permit, but worth every effort).

9. **Saguaro National Park**—Stroll among towering saguaro cacti in this desert utopia.

10. **Meteor Crater**—Visit a perfectly preserved impact crater from 50,000 years ago.

11. **Desert Botanical Garden**—Walk through a desert garden with 50,000 plants spread over 140 acres.

12. **Grand Canyon Village**—Visit a village dating back to the 20th century.

13. **Camelback Mountain**—Hike and climb a formation resembling a camel's hump.

Adventures for Thrill-Seekers

14. **Rim-to-Rim Hike of the Grand Canyon**—Conquer one of the nation's most iconic hikes.

15. **Kayaking on Lake Powell**—Paddle through hidden canyons and crystal-clear waters.

16. **Hot Air Balloon Ride Over Phoenix**—See the Sonoran Desert from the sky at dawn.

17. **Stargazing and Astronomy Whitewater Rafting the Colorado River**—Feel the intensity of nature in the Grand Canyon's roaring rapids.

18. **Skydiving Over Arizona's Desert**—Get your adrenaline fix paired with unbeatable views.

Iconic Cultural Landmarks

19. **Taliesin West**—Tour Frank Lloyd Wright's architectural masterpiece.

20. **Mission San Xavier del Bac**—Admire this stunning 18th-century Spanish mission outside Tucson.

21. **Old Town Scottsdale**—Shop artisan crafts and experience cowboy heritage.

22. **The Heard Museum**—Dive deep into Native American art and culture.

23. **Route 66 (Winslow, Arizona)**—Stand on a corner and relive the magic of this historic highway.

Stargazing & Astronomy

24. **Lowell Observatory**—Discover the stars at the site where Pluto was first identified.

25. **Kitt Peak National Observatory**—Peer into the universe from one of the world's finest telescope facilities.

26. **Sedona's Night Sky**—International Dark-Sky Community? Prepare to lose yourself in an infinite blanket of stars.

27. **Flagstaff Dark Skies**—Officially certified as a dark-sky city for prime stargazing.

28. **Meteor Shower in the Desert**—Plan your trip during the Perseids for an unforgettable night.

Unique Local Experiences

29. **Tombstone**—Step back in time in this famed Wild West town.

30. **Bisbee**—Wander through an artistic community housed within a charming mining town.

31. **Arizona Wine Country (Verde Valley)**—Sip local vintages while enjoying pastoral landscapes.

32. **Santa Cruz Chili & Spice Co.**—Indulge in the rich culinary traditions of the Southwest.

33. **Sunset Crater Volcano National Monument**—Explore the lava fields of Arizona's volcanic past.

Awe-Inspiring Road Trips

34. **Apache Trail**—Drive a scenic dirt road adventure past lakes, canyons, and cliffside views.

35. **Vermilion Cliffs National Monument**—Feel dwarfed by towering sandstone cliffs.

36. **Mogollon Rim**—Travel along this plateau's edge for unparalleled vistas.

37. **Jerome's Skyway**—Cruise through Arizona's famous "ghost town turned art hub."

38. **Chiricahua National Monument**—Take in a land of sky-high, precariously balanced rock spires.

39. **Monument Valley**—Take a surreal drive through towering red sandstone formations.

40. **Sedona's Red Rock Scenic Byway**—Drive this route through Sedona's glowing red cliffs and buttes.

41. **Petrified Forest National Park**—Drive through fossilized trees and vibrant badlands.

42. **Mount Lemmon Scenic Byway**—Drive this 27-mile road from desert landscapes to alpine forests.

43. **Lake Powell and Glen Canyon**—See where water meets sandstone, creating breathtaking scenic contrasts.

Off-the-Beaten-Path Gems

44. **Canyon de Chelly National Monument**—Explore this sacred Navajo site with towering canyon walls.

45. **Tumacácori National Historical Park**—Visit these preserved Spanish mission ruins.

46. **Kartchner Caverns State Park**—Step into Arizona's best-preserved underground caves.

47. **Organ Pipe Cactus National Monument**—Walk among rare cacti on Mexico's border.

48. **Essence of Tranquility**—Explore a hot springs retreat offering six mineral-rich pools.

Wellness & Reflection

49. **Sedona's Vortex Hikes**—Recharge at one of the city's spiritual energy spots.

50. **Page's Lake Powell Paddleboarding**—Find serenity skimming across still waters.

51. **A Day at Marble Canyon Ranch**—Relax amid spectacular views paired with horseback riding or fly fishing.

www.ingramcontent.com/pod-product-compliance
Lightning Source LLC
Chambersburg PA
CBHW081743220526
45468CB00008B/2217